STUDENT FINANCIAL HELP

Student Financial Help
A GUIDE TO MONEY FOR COLLEGE

Louis T. and Joyce W. Scaringi

Dolphin Books

DOUBLEDAY & COMPANY, INC.
Garden City, New York
1974

LIBRARY OF CONGRESS CATALOGING IN PUBLICATION DATA

SCARINGI, LOUIS T 1925–
STUDENT FINANCIAL HELP.

1. STUDENT AID—UNITED STATES. I. SCARINGI,
JOYCE W., 1929– JOINT AUTHOR. II. TITLE.
LB2337.4.S28   378.3'0973
ISBN 0-385-01977-7
LIBRARY OF CONGRESS CATALOG CARD NUMBER 73–16513

CONTENTS

Part II: SELECTED NONFEDERAL UNDERGRADUATE
STUDENT ASSISTANCE PROGRAMS   39

Part III: SELECTED STATE UNDERGRADUATE STUDENT
ASSISTANCE PROGRAMS   65

Part I

SELECTED FEDERAL UNDERGRADUATE STUDENT ASSISTANCE PROGRAMS

1. GUARANTEED–STUDENT LOAN PROGRAM

PROVIDES for low-interest deferred loans for students attending nearly four thousand eligible institutions of higher education and nursing both in the United States and abroad and approximately thirty-five hundred vocational, technical, business, correspondence, and trade schools. The principal amount of the loan is provided by participating lending institutions, i.e., commercial banks, savings and loan associations, credit unions, insurance companies, pension funds, and eligible educational institutions. The loan is insured by a state or private nonprofit agency or the federal government.

ELIGIBILITY. Regardless of family income, any student is eligible for a guaranteed loan if he is enrolled (or accepted for enrollment) as at least a half-time student. A student who provides the lender with a statement from his school evidencing his need for a loan may also apply for interest benefits, which pay the interest on the loan while the student is in school and for a grace period of nine to twelve months thereafter. (Vocational students do not need an elementary or high school diploma and may attend any business, technical, trade, or other vocational school approved for this program).

AMOUNT OF ASSISTANCE. A student may borrow up to $2,500 per academic year, with a maximum unpaid principal of $7,500 for undergraduates and $10,000 for graduate or professional students.

The repayment period usually begins nine to twelve months after the student finishes school, or leaves school, or ceases to carry at least one half of an academic workload. Repayments are usually made over a period of from five to ten years requiring a minimum monthly payment of $30. During repayment, the student pays the total interest of 7 percent, plus an insurance premium of either ¼ percent under the federal program or ½ percent under the state and private programs.

Repayment may generally be deferred up to three years if the borrower is serving on active duty in the Armed Forces, Peace Corps, or VISTA, or for any period during which he is a full-time student in any eligible institution.

WHERE TO APPLY. Applications for guaranteed student loans may be obtained from lenders, schools, state and federal agencies, or private nonprofit agencies. The school must verify the student's enrollment or acceptance and also certify the costs involved and good standing of the student. The application form is then presented to a participating bank or other suitable lender. For information regarding the operation of the guaranteed loan program within your state, contact the appropriate agency listed below:

Sources of Information on the Guaranteed Loan Programs for Students

ALABAMA
    Director of Higher Education
    Office of Education, Region IV
    50 Seventh Street, N.E.
    Atlanta, Georgia 30323

ALASKA
    Student Aid Office
    State Education Department
    Pouch F, AOB
    Juneau, Alaska 99801

ARIZONA
    Director of Higher Education
    Office of Education, Region IX
    50 Fulton Street
    San Francisco, California 94102

ARKANSAS
Student Loan Guarantee
Foundation of Arkansas
Suite 515, 1515 W. 7th Street
Little Rock, Arkansas 72202

CALIFORNIA
Director of Higher Education
Office of Education, Region IX
50 Fulton Street
San Francisco, California 94102

COLORADO
Director of Higher Education
Office of Education, Region VIII
Room 9017, Federal Office Building
19th and Stout Streets
Denver, Colorado 80202

CONNECTICUT
Connecticut Student Loan Foundation
251 Asylum Street
Hartford, Connecticut 06103

DELAWARE
Delaware Higher Education Loan
Program
% Brandywine College
P. O. Box 7139
Wilmington, Delaware 19803

DISTRICT OF COLUMBIA
D. C. Student Loan Insurance
Program
1329 E. Street, N.W.
Washington, D.C. 20004

FLORIDA
Director of Higher Education
Office of Education, Region IV
50 Seventh Street, N.E.
Atlanta, Georgia 30323

GEORGIA
Georgia Higher Education
Assistance Corporation
P. O. Box 38005
Capitol Hill Station
Atlanta, Georgia 30339

HAWAII
Director of Higher Education
Office of Education, Region IX
50 Fulton Street
San Francisco, California 94102

IDAHO
Director of Higher Education
Office of Education, Region X
Arcade Plaza Building
1321 Second Avenue
Seattle, Washington 98101

ILLINOIS
Illinois State Scholarship Commission
730 Waukegan Road
Deerfield, Illinois 60015

INDIANA
Director of Higher Education
Office of Education, Region V
226 West Jackson Boulevard
Chicago, Illinois 60606

IOWA
Director of Higher Education
Office of Education, Region VII
601 East 12th Street
Kansas City, Missouri 64106

KANSAS
Director of Higher Education
Office of Education, Region VII
601 East 12th Street
Kansas City, Missouri 64106

KENTUCKY
Director of Higher Education
Office of Education, Region IV
50 Seventh Street, N.E.
Atlanta, Georgia 30323

LOUISIANA (in-state students)
Louisiana Higher Education
Assistance Commission
Box 44095, Capitol Station
Baton Rouge, Louisiana 70804

LOUISIANA (out-of-state students)
United Student Aid Funds, Inc.
845 Third Avenue
New York, New York 10022

MAINE
Maine State Department of Education
Augusta, Maine 04330

MARYLAND
Maryland Higher Education Loan
Corporation
2100 Guilford Avenue
Baltimore, Maryland 21218

MASSACHUSETTS
Massachusetts Higher Education
Assistance Corporation
511 Statler Building
Boston, Massachusetts 02116

MICHIGAN
Michigan Higher Education
Assistance Authority
Second Floor, Leonard Building
309 North Washington Avenue
Lansing, Michigan 48902

MINNESOTA
Director of Higher Education
Office of Education, Region V
300 South Wacker Drive
Chicago, Illinois 60606

MISSISSIPPI
Director of Higher Education
Office of Education, Region IV
50 Seventh Street, N.E.
Atlanta, Georgia 30323

MISSOURI
Director of Higher Education
Office of Education, Region VII
601 East 12th Street
Kansas City, Missouri 64106

MONTANA
Director of Higher Education
Office of Education, Region VIII
9017 Federal Office Building
19th and Stout Streets
Denver, Colorado 80202

NEBRASKA
Director of Higher Education
Office of Education, Region VII
601 East 12th Street
Kansas City, Missouri 64106

NEVADA
Deputy Superintendent and
Coordinator of Divisions
Nevada State Department of Education
Carson City, Nevada 78901

NEW HAMPSHIRE
New Hampshire Higher Education
Assistance Foundation
3 Capitol Street
Concord, New Hampshire 03301

NEW JERSEY
New Jersey Higher Education
Assistance Authority
65 Prospect Street
Trenton, New Jersey 08625

NEW MEXICO
Director of Higher Education
Office of Education, Region VI
1114 Commerce Street
Dallas, Texas 75202

NEW YORK
New York Higher Education
Assistance Corporation
50 Wolf Road
Albany, New York 12205

NORTH CAROLINA
State Education Assistance Authority
P. O. Box 2688, Chapel Hill
Chapel Hill, North Carolina 27514

NORTH DAKOTA
Director of Higher Education
Office of Education, Region VIII
Room 9017, Federal Office Building
19th and Stout Streets
Denver, Colorado 80202

OHIO
Ohio Student Loan Commission
33 North High Street
Columbus, Ohio 43215

OKLAHOMA
Oklahoma State Regents for Higher
Education
State Capitol Station, Box 43383
Oklahoma City, Oklahoma 73105

OREGON
State of Oregon Scholarship
Commission
1445 Willamette Street
Eugene, Oregon 97402

PENNSYLVANIA
Pennsylvania Higher Education
Assistance Agency
Towne House, 660 Boas Street
Harrisburg, Pennsylvania 17102

PUERTO RICO
Director of Higher Education
Office of Education, Region II
26 Federal Plaza
New York, New York 10007

RHODE ISLAND
Rhode Island Higher Education
Assistance Corporation
187 Westminster Mall
Room 414, Box 579
Providence, Rhode Island 02901

SOUTH CAROLINA
United Student Aid Funds, Inc.
845 Third Avenue
New York, New York 10022

SOUTH DAKOTA
Director of Higher Education
Office of Education, Region VIII
19th and Stout Streets
Denver, Colorado 80202

TENNESSEE
Tennessee Education Loan
Corporation
State Department of Education
313 Capitol Towers
Nashville, Tennessee 37219

TEXAS
Director of Higher Education
Office of Education, Region VI
1114 Commerce Street
Dallas, Texas 75202

UTAH
Director of Higher Education
Office of Education, Region VIII
Room 9017, Federal Office Building
19th and Stout Streets
Denver, Colorado 80202

VERMONT
Vermont Student Assistance
Corporation
156 College Street
Burlington, Vermont 05401

VIRGINIA
Virginia State Education Assistance
Authority
501 East Franklin Street
Suite 311, Professional Building
Richmond, Virginia 23219

VIRGIN ISLANDS
United Student Aid Funds, Inc.
845 Third Avenue
New York, New York 10022

WASHINGTON
Director of Higher Education
Office of Education, Region X
Arcade Plaza Building
1321 Second Avenue
Seattle, Washington 98101

WEST VIRGINIA
Director of Higher Education
Office of Education, Region III
P. O. Box 13716
3535 Market Street
Philadelphia, Pennsylvania 19101

WISCONSIN
Wisconsin Higher Education
Corporation
State Office Building
115 West Wilson Street
Madison, Wisconsin 53702

WYOMING
Director of Higher Education
Office of Education, Region VIII
Room 9017, Federal Office Building
19th and Stout Streets
Denver, Colorado 80202

2. UNITED STUDENT AID FUNDS LOAN PROGRAM

United Student Aid Funds, Inc.
5259 North Tacoma Avenue
Indianapolis, Indiana 46220

PROVIDES long-term low-cost educational loans that are guaranteed to the lender by United Student Aid Funds, Inc., in case of death or default on the part of the student borrower. The United Student Aid Fund Loan Program can be particularly useful to students whose colleges do not have enough loan funds, or to students from middle-income families who may not qualify for assistance elsewhere.

This program is similar to the Guaranteed Student Loan Program described in the preceding section. Each state has a student loan guarantee plan for its residents. Some are operated by a state agency, while other states have designated United Student Aid Funds to operate their programs.

ELIGIBILITY. Regardless of family income, any student is eligible for a guaranteed loan if he is enrolled (or accepted for enrollment) as at least a half-time student. (For a student who qualifies under federal law, the federal government will pay the interest while he is in school and during authorized periods when repayment is not required.)

AMOUNT OF ASSISTANCE. Amount of assistance and repayment provisions are also similar to the Guaranteed Student Loan Program described in the preceding section.

WHERE TO APPLY. Application information may be obtained from the financial aid officer of the college the student plans to attend, or from:

3. COLLEGE WORK-STUDY PROGRAM

PROVIDES part-time employment opportunities for needy students pursuing a course of study at an eligible postsecondary institution.

ELIGIBILITY. Determined by the financial aid officer of participating institutions of higher education. The student must be enrolled (or accepted for enrollment) at least half-time and in need of the earnings from part-time employment under this program to pursue a course of study at the institution. Students in eligible area vocational schools are eligible, as are students at eligible proprietary, postsecondary, secretarial, and business schools. A student in a proprietary school may work for public or private nonprofit organizations, but not for the school in which enrolled.)

AMOUNT OF ASSISTANCE. Salary paid is at least equal to the current minimum wage, although frequently higher for as many as forty hours weekly, or such lesser hours as determined by the financial aid officer (In addition, students may also receive a nonfederal loan as well as a National Direct Student Loan or Supplemental Educational Opportunity Grant, if determined eligible by the financial aid officer.)

WHERE TO APPLY. Most postsecondary institutions participate in this program. The federal government currently provides 80 percent of student earnings, while participating colleges and universities arrange for the other 20 percent.

13

Application is made to the institution the student plans to enter. Further information may be obtained from the student financial aid office at the college the student plans to attend.

4. COOPERATIVE EDUCATION (WORK-STUDY) PROGRAM

PROVIDES college credit to a student while working full-time in the occupation of his choice for part of the academic year. He then spends the rest of the school year as a full-time student.

ELIGIBILITY. Any student enrolled (or accepted for enrollment) is eligible, although some of the participating schools restrict enrollment to honor students.

AMOUNT OF ASSISTANCE. Assistance is in the form of granting college credit to the student for the part of the academic year during which he is working full-time.

WHERE TO APPLY. Application information may be obtained by writing to the admissions office of the institution the student plans to attend.

5. NATIONAL DIRECT STUDENT LOANS

PROVIDE long-term, low-interest educational loans to qualified students.

ELIGIBILITY. Determined by the financial aid officer of participating institutions of higher education. Students in eligible postsecondary secretarial and business schools are also eligible. The student must be in need of the amount of his loan to pursue his course of study in the institution, and must be enrolled (or accepted for enrollment) as at least a half-time student.

AMOUNT OF ASSISTANCE. A student may borrow up to $5,000 to complete undergraduate study leading to a bachelor's degree. (There are also provisions for graduate and professional students.) The repayment period and interest do not begin until nine months after a student ends his studies or ceases at least half-time study. Loans are charged interest at the rate of 3 percent on the unpaid balance, and repayment of principal may be extended over a ten-year period. Repayment can also be deferred or canceled in the following cases:

1. *Deferred payment.* No repayment is required and no interest is charged for any period up to three years during which you are serving in the Armed Forces, Peace Corps, or VISTA, or are continuing your education in another institution of higher education as at least a half-time student.

2. *Cancellation of loan.* If the borrower becomes a teacher in a designated low-income-area elementary or secondary school, or teaches handicapped children in an elementary or secondary school system, 100 percent of the loan (plus interest) may be canceled, at the rate of 15 percent for the first and second years, 20 percent for the third and fourth years, and 30 percent for the fifth year, of the amount owed upon entering teaching.

   If the borrower becomes a full-time professional member in a Head-Start program, the loan (plus interest) may be canceled at the rate of 15 percent for each year.

   If the borrower enters the military service, loans made after July 1, 1972, may be canceled at the rate of 12½ percent of the total (plus interest) for each year of consecutive military service (not to exceed 50 percent of the total loan) for which the borrower qualifies for combat pay.

WHERE TO APPLY. Application is made to the institution the student plans to enter. Most postsecondary institutions participate in this program. The federal government provides 90 percent of each student loan. Participating colleges and universities provide the other 10 percent.

6. SUPPLEMENTAL EDUCATIONAL OPPORTUNITY GRANTS PROGRAM

PROVIDES assistance in the form of outright grants to high school graduates of exceptional financial need who, without these grants, would be unable to attend college.

ELIGIBILITY. Determined by financial aid officer of participating institutions. The student must be enrolled (or accepted for enrollment) as an undergraduate on at least a half-time basis. A superior academic record is not a requirement.

AMOUNT OF ASSISTANCE. Students may receive grants of $200 to $1,500 per academic year for four years of undergraduate studies. The amount of the grant, which does not have to be repaid, is determined by the participating institution.

WHERE TO APPLY. Application is made to the institution the student plans to enter. Most postsecondary institutions participate in this program.

7. NURSING STUDENT FEDERAL LOANS AND SCHOLARSHIPS PROGRAM

PROVIDES long-term, low-interest loans and scholarships to qualified students through accredited participating schools of nursing, under the Nurse Training Act of 1971.

LOANS

ELIGIBILITY. Students who are citizens of the United States or have been admitted as permanent residents, and who are enrolled (or accepted for enrollment) full-time or half-time in a course of study leading to a diploma in nursing, an associate degree in nursing, a bachelor's degree (or equivalent) in nursing, or a graduate degree in nursing are eligible.

AMOUNT OF ASSISTANCE. A student may borrow up to $2,500 per academic year, with a maximum total of $10,000 for all years. Loans (plus 3 percent interest) are repayable over a ten-year period beginning nine months after the student leaves school. Repayment may be deferred or subject to partial cancellation under the following conditions:

1. *Deferred payment.* Payment may be deferred up to three years during periods of active duty in a uniformed service or as a volunteer in the Peace Corps; up to five years during periods of full-time advanced nursing study.

2. *Cancellation.* Up to 85 percent of a federal nursing loan plus interest may be canceled for three to five years of employment as a registered nurse in a public or nonprofit private institution, agency, or organization; up to 85 percent of all loans (plus interest) for nursing education may, under agreement with the Secretary of Health, Education, and Welfare, be canceled for two to three years of employment in an identified area of nursing shortage.

15

SCHOLARSHIPS

ELIGIBILITY. Students who are citizens of the United States or have been admitted as permanent residents, and who are enrolled (or accepted for enrollment) full-time or half-time in a course of study leading to a diploma in nursing, an associate degree in nursing, a bachelor's degree (or equivalent) in nursing, or a graduate degree in nursing, are eligible.

AMOUNT OF ASSISTANCE. A student may be awarded a scholarship of up to $2,000 per year, dependent upon the availability of funds and the student's financial need as determined by the nursing school.

WHERE TO APPLY. Application (for loans and scholarships) should be made to the institution the student plans to enter. Further information (and a list of participating institutions) may be obtained from;

Division of Nursing
Bureau of Health Manpower Education
National Institutes of Health
Bethesda, Maryland 20014

8. THE GI BILL (EDUCATION BENEFITS)

PROVIDES educational and training allowances for qualified veterans and servicemen. Generally provides 36 months (4 years of college) of educational assistance for those who served on active duty for 18 months or longer after January 31, 1955. For those with less than 18 months service, it provides 1½ months of educational assistance for each month of service.

ELIGIBILITY. Veterans and servicemen who have served over 180 days on active duty, any part of which occurred after January 31, 1955, or who were discharged after that date inside of 180 days because of disability incurred while on active duty, are eligible.

AMOUNT OF ASSISTANCE. Full-time students receive an allowance amount of $220 per month for each month of active duty up to 36 academic months (4 years of college). Additional allowances for dependents are received at the rate of $41 for the first dependent, $37 for the second, and $18 for each dependent in excess of 2. Students enrolled less than full-time receive smaller benefits. Allowance amounts are as follows:

| | | Dependents | | |
| | | | | Each |
	No	One	Two	Add.
Full-time	$220	$261	$298	$18
Three-quarter time	165	196	224	14
Half-time	110	131	149	9

(Dependent: wife, child, or dependent parent)

WHERE TO APPLY. Application information may be obtained from the nearest Veterans' Administration office in your area. (Check your telephone directory under the heading, "U. S. Government.")

9. DEPENDENTS' EDUCATIONAL ASSISTANCE PROGRAM (CHILDREN)

PROVIDES educational and training allowances for a period of thirty-six months (four years of college) for children of certain veterans.

ELIGIBILITY. Sons and daughters between eighteen and twenty-six years of age (whether single or married) who are children of veterans who died or are permanently and totally disabled as a result of service in the Armed Forces, and children of servicemen held as prisoners of war (POW) or listed as MIA (missing in action) for a total of more than ninety days, are eligible. Benefits stop when the eligible student reaches age twenty-six, unless extended under one or more of the following conditions (in no event will assistance be accorded beyond age thirty-one):

1. For those eligible children who serve in the Armed Forces between their eighteenth and twenty-sixth birthdays, the period of eligibility is extended for five years after discharge or release from active duty.

2. For those eligible children who were below age twenty-six when the Veterans' Pension and Readjustment Assistance Act of 1967 became effective (August 31, 1967), eligibility will continue until September 30, 1972.

3. For those eligible children whose veteran parent died or was first found to be permanently and totally disabled after the eligible child's eighteenth but before his twenty-sixth birthday, the period of eligibility will end five years after the date of such death or date the permanent and total disability was first determined.

4. Certain other conditions occurring after the eligible child was enrolled in courses under this program, and that were beyond his control as determined by the Veterans' Administration.

AMOUNT OF ASSISTANCE. The eligible student receives a monthly allowance of $220 if he is a full-time student. For those students who are less than full-time, smaller allowances are available.

WHERE TO APPLY. Application information can be obtained from the nearest Veterans' Administration office in your area. (Check your telephone directory under the heading, "U. S. Government.")

10. DEPENDENTS' EDUCATIONAL ASSISTANCE PROGRAM (WIVES AND WIDOWS)

PROVIDES educational and training allowances for a period of thirty-six months (four years of college) for widows of veterans who died as a result of service-related causes and for wives of veterans who are permanently and totally disabled as a result of military service, or held as prisoners of war (POW) or listed as missing in action (MIA).

ELIGIBILITY. Widows of veterans who died of service-related causes, and wives of veterans who are permanently and totally disabled as a result of military service are eligible, as are wives of servicemen held as POWs or listed as MIA for a total of more than ninety days. Such wives and widows have a wide choice of educational programs such as attending college, vocational, business or technical schools, etc. A widow must use her entitlement within eight years after her veteran husband's death, and a wife must use her entitlement within eight years after her veteran husband is found to be totally disabled. However, all eligible wives and widows have up to November 30, 1976, as a minimum, to take advantage of these educational benefits.

Widows who remarry and wives who divorce their permanently and totally disabled veteran husbands lose their eligibility. However, the remarried widow regains her rights upon termination of the remarriage.

AMOUNT OF ASSISTANCE. The eligible widow or wife receives a monthly allowance of $220 if enrolled as a full-time student. For those enrolled as less than full-time, smaller allowances are available subject to the original eight-year eligibility period.

WHERE TO APPLY. Application information may be obtained from the nearest Veterans' Administration office in your area. (Check your telephone directory under the heading, "U. S. Government.")

11. U. S. MILITARY ACADEMY PROGRAM

PROVIDES four-year scholarship (plus monthly allowance) to the U. S. Military Academy at West Point, New York.

ELIGIBILITY. Unmarried male students between the ages of seventeen and twenty-two who can meet competitive academic and physical entrance requirements are eligible. Nominations are made by the U.S. senators and representatives of your state. The U. S. Military Academy confers a B.S. degree, and graduates are commissioned as regular officers in the U. S. Army.

AMOUNT OF ASSISTANCE. Students receive tuition, room, board, and medical and dental care, plus a monthly allowance (from which he pays for uniforms, textbooks, and living incidentals).

WHERE TO APPLY. Application information may be obtained from your high school counselor, or by writing to:

Director of Admissions
United States Military Academy
West Point, New York 10996

12. U. S. NAVAL ACADEMY PROGRAM

PROVIDES four-year scholarship (plus monthly allowance) to the U. S. Naval Academy at Annapolis, Maryland.

ELIGIBILITY. Unmarried male students between the ages of seventeen and twenty-two who can meet competitive academic and physical entrance requirements are eligible. Nominations are made by the U.S. senators and representatives of your state. The U. S. Naval Academy confers a B.S. degree, and graduates are commissioned as regular officers in the U. S. Navy or Marine Corps.

AMOUNT OF ASSISTANCE. Students receive tuition, room, board, and medical and dental care, plus a monthly allowance (from which he pays for uniforms, textbooks, and living incidentals).

WHERE TO APPLY. Application information may be obtained from your high school counselor, or by writing to:

Dean of Admissions
United States Naval Academy
Annapolis, Maryland 21421

13. U. S. AIR FORCE ACADEMY PROGRAM

PROVIDES four-year scholarship (plus monthly allowance) to the U. S. Air Force Academy at Colorado Springs, Colorado.

ELIGIBILITY. Unmarried male students between the ages of seventeen and twenty-two who can meet competitive academic and physical entrance requirements are eligible. Nominations are made by the

U.S. senators and representatives of your state. The U. S. Air Force Academy confers a B.S. degree, and graduates are commissioned as regular officers in the U. S. Air Force.

AMOUNT OF ASSISTANCE. Students receive their education, room, board, and medical and dental care plus a monthly allowance (from which he pays for uniforms, textbooks, and living incidentals).

WHERE TO APPLY. Application information may be obtained from your high school counselor, or by writing to:

Office of the Registrar (RRV)
United States Air Force Academy
Colorado Springs, Colorado 80840

14. U. S. MERCHANT MARINE ACADEMY PROGRAM

PROVIDES four-year scholarship (plus allowance) to the U. S. Merchant Marine Academy at Kings Point, New York.

ELIGIBILITY. Unmarried students between the ages of seventeen and twenty-two who can meet competitive academic and physical entrance requirements are eligible. Nominations are made by the U.S. senators and representatives of your state. Upon successful completion of the four-year course, students receive a B.S. degree and a commission as ensign in the U. S. Naval Reserve.

AMOUNT OF ASSISTANCE. Students receive tuition, room, board, and medical and dental care, plus allowance (which defrays costs of uniforms and textbooks).

WHERE TO APPLY. Application information may be obtained from your high school counselor, or by writing to:

Director of Admissions
United States Merchant Marine Academy
Kings Point, New York 11024

15. U. S. COAST GUARD ACADEMY PROGRAM

PROVIDES four-year scholarship (plus monthly allowance) to the U. S. Coast Guard Academy at New London, Connecticut.

ELIGIBILITY. Unmarried male students between the ages of seventeen and twenty-two who can meet competitive academic and physical entrance requirements are eligible. Upon successful completion of the four-year course, students receive a B.S. degree and a commission as ensign in the U. S. Coast Guard.

AMOUNT OF ASSISTANCE. Students receive tuition, room, board, medical and dental care, and a monthly allowance (from which he pays for uniforms, textbooks, and other items necessary for his training), plus a subsistence allowance.

WHERE TO APPLY. Students should follow application procedures similar to those for a "civilian" college. Application is made to:

Director of Admissions
United States Coast Guard Academy
New London, Connecticut 06320

16. RESERVE OFFICER TRAINING CORPS SCHOLARSHIP PROGRAM (U. S. ARMY)

PROVIDES four-year scholarship (plus monthly allowance while in school) to a participating college or university hosting the program. (Students reaching their senior year of college also have an opportunity to learn to fly. This Army ROTC Flight Instruction Program is optional and consists of approximately 35 hours of ground instruction and 36½ hours of in-flight instruction.)

ELIGIBILITY. Any student (at least seventeen years of age and a U.S. citizen) who is acceptable for enrollment in one of the participating colleges or universities is eligible for the competitive four-year scholarship, which will lead to a commission in the Regular Army or the Army Reserve, whichever is offered. The student must be able to complete all requirements for a college degree and a commission prior to attaining age twenty-five.

(Three- and two-year scholarships are also available, but only to students already enrolled in ROTC.)

AMOUNT OF ASSISTANCE. Selected students receive tuition, fees, laboratory expenses, books, and a monthly allowance of $100 per month for up to ten months of each school year.

WHERE TO APPLY. Request for applications must be submitted by December 1 for the following school year. Applications and further information can be obtained from:

Army ROTC Scholarships
P. O. Box 12703
Philadelphia, Pennsylvania 19134

Colleges and Universities conducting the Army ROTC Scholarship Program are listed below:

ALABAMA
Alabama A and M University
Auburn University
Florence State University
Jacksonville State University
*Marion Institute
Spring Hill College
Tuskegee Institute
University of Alabama

University of South Alabama
ALASKA
University of Alaska
ARIZONA
Arizona State University
University of Arizona
ARKANSAS
Arkansas Polytechnic College
Arkansas State University
Henderson State College
Ouachita Baptist University
Southern State College
State College of Arkansas
University of Arkansas, Fayetteville
University of Arkansas, Pine Bluff
CALIFORNIA
California Polytechnic State University
California State University, San Jose
The Claremont Colleges
University of California, Berkeley
University of California, Davis
University of California, Los Angeles
University of California, Santa Barbara
University of San Francisco
University of Santa Clara
COLORADO
Colorado College
Colorado School of Mines
Colorado State University
Southern Colorado State College
University of Colorado
CONNECTICUT
University of Connecticut, Storrs
University of Connecticut, Hartford Branch
University of Connecticut, Waterbury Branch
DELAWARE
University of Delaware
DISTRICT OF COLUMBIA
Georgetown University
Howard University
FLORIDA
Florida A and M University

denotes a military junior college

20

Florida Institute of Technology
Florida Southern College
Florida State University
Stetson University
University of Florida
University of Miami
University of Tampa

GEORGIA
Columbus College
Fort Valley State College
Georgia Institute of Technology
*Georgia Military College
Georgia State University
Mercer University
North Georgia College
University of Georgia

HAWAII
University of Hawaii

IDAHO
Boise State College
Idaho State University
University of Idaho

ILLINOIS
DePaul University
Knox College
Loyola University
Northern Illinois University
University of Illinois
University of Illinois, Chicago Circle Campus
Western Illinois University
Wheaton College

INDIANA
Indiana Institute of Technology
Indiana University
Purdue University
Rose-Hulman Institute of Technology
University of Notre Dame

IOWA
Iowa State University of S and T
University of Iowa

KANSAS
Kansas State College of Pittsburg
Kansas State University of A and AS

University of Kansas
Wichita State University

KENTUCKY
Eastern Kentucky University
Morehead State University
Murray State University
University of Kentucky
Western Kentucky University

LOUISIANA
Louisiana State University and A and M College
Loyola University
McNeese State College
Nicholls State College
Northeast Louisiana University
Northwestern State College of Louisiana
Southeastern Louisiana College
Southern University and A and M College
Tulane University

MAINE
Bowdoin College
University of Maine

MARYLAND
Loyola College
Morgan State College
The Johns Hopkins University
Western Maryland College

MASSACHUSETTS
Massachusetts Institute of Technology
Northeastern University
University of Massachusetts
Worcester Polytechnic Institute

MICHIGAN
Central Michigan University
Eastern Michigan University
Lake Superior State College
Michigan State University
Michigan Technological University
Northern Michigan University
University of Detroit
University of Michigan
Western Michigan University

denotes a military junior college

21

MINNESOTA
St. John's University
University of Minnesota

MISSISSIPPI
Alcorn A and M College
Jackson State College
Mississippi State University
University of Mississippi
University of Southern Mississippi

MISSOURI
Central Missouri State College
*Kemper Military School and College
Lincoln University
Missouri Western College
Northeast Missouri State College
Southwest Missouri State College
University of Missouri at Columbia
University of Missouri at Rolla
Washington University, St. Louis
*Wentworth Military Academy and
    Junior College
Westminster College

MONTANA
Montana State University
University of Montana

NEBRASKA
Kearney State College
The Creighton University
University of Nebraska

NEVADA
University of Nevada

NEW HAMPSHIRE
University of New Hampshire

NEW JERSEY
Princeton University
Rider College
Rutgers University
St. Peter's College
Seton Hall University

NEW MEXICO
Eastern New Mexico University
*New Mexico Military Institute
New Mexico State University

NEW YORK
Alfred University
Canisius College
Clarkson College of Technology
Cornell University
Fordham University
Hofstra University
Niagara University
Polytechnic Institute of Brooklyn
Rensselaer Polytechnic Institute
Rochester Institute of Technology
St. Bonaventure University
St. John's University
St. Lawrence University
Siena College
Syracuse University

NORTH CAROLINA
Appalachian State University
Campbell College
Davidson College
North Carolina A and T State University
North Carolina State University at Raleigh
Wake Forest University

NORTH DAKOTA
North Dakota State University of A
    and AS
University of North Dakota

OHIO
Bowling Green State University
Central State University
John Carroll University
Kent State University
Ohio State University
Ohio University
University of Akron
University of Cincinnati
University of Dayton
University of Toledo
Xavier University
Youngstown State University

OKLAHOMA
Cameron College
Central State College

denotes a military junior college

22

East Central State College
Northwestern State College
Oklahoma State University
Panhandle State College
Southwestern State College
University of Oklahoma

OREGON
Oregon State University
University of Oregon

PENNSYLVANIA
Bucknell University
Carnegie-Mellon University
Dickinson College
Drexel Institute of Technology
Duquesne University
Gannon College
Gettysburg College
Indiana University of Pennsylvania
Lafayette College
LaSalle College
Lehigh University
Pennsylvania State University
Pennsylvania State University at Abington
Pennsylvania State University at Altoona
Pennsylvania State University at Chester
Pennsylvania State University at Schuylkill Haven
Temple University
University of Pennsylvania
University of Pittsburgh
University of Scranton
*Valley Forge Military Academy
Washington and Jefferson College
Widener College

PUERTO RICO
University of Puerto Rico, Mayaguez Campus
University of Puerto Rico, Rio Piedras Campus

RHODE ISLAND
Providence College

University of Rhode Island

SOUTH CAROLINA
Clemson University
Furman University
Presbyterian College
South Carolina State College
The Citadel
Wofford College

SOUTH DAKOTA
South Dakota School of Mines and Technology
South Dakota State University
University of South Dakota

TENNESSEE
Austin-Peay State University
Carson-Newman College
East Tennessee State University
Middle Tennessee State University
Tennessee Technological University
University of Tennessee
University of Tennessee at Chattanooga
University of Tennessee at Martin
Vanderbilt University

TEXAS
Bishop College
Hardin-Simmons University
Midwestern University
Prairie View A and M College
Rice University
St. Mary's University of San Antonio
Sam Houston State University
Stephen F. Austin State College
Tarleton State College
Texas A and I University
Texas A and M University
Texas Christian University
Texas Tech. University
Trinity University
University of Houston
University of Texas
University of Texas at Arlington
University of Texas at El Paso
West Texas State University

* denotes a military junior college

23

UTAH
  Brigham Young University
  University of Utah
  Utah State University
  Weber State College

VERMONT
  Middlebury College
  Norwich University
  University of Vermont

VIRGINIA
  Hampton Institute
  Norfolk State College
  Old Dominion University
  The College of William and Mary
  University of Richmond
  University of Virginia
  Virginia Military Institute
  Virginia Polytechnic Institute and State
    University
  Virginia State College
  Washington and Lee University

WASHINGTON
  Eastern Washington State College
  Gonzaga University
  Seattle University
  University of Washington
  Washington State University

WEST VIRGINIA
  Marshall University
  Potomac State College
  West Virginia State College
  West Virginia University

WISCONSIN
  Marquette University
  Ripon College
  St. Norbert College
  University of Wisconsin, La Crosse
  University of Wisconsin, Madison
  University of Wisconsin, Milwaukee
  University of Wisconsin, Oshkosh
  University of Wisconsin, Platteville
  University of Wisconsin, Stevens Point
  University of Wisconsin, Whitewater

WYOMING
  University of Wyoming

17. RESERVE OFFICER TRAINING CORPS SCHOLARSHIP PROGRAM (U. S. NAVY)

PROVIDES four-year scholarship (plus monthly allowance) to a participating college or university.

ELIGIBILITY. Students between the ages of seventeen and twenty-one are eligible for the competitive four-year scholarship, which will lead to a commission as ensign in the U. S. Navy or as a second lieutenant in the U. S. Marine Corps.

(Three- and two-year scholarships are also available, but only to students already enrolled in Navy ROTC.)

AMOUNT OF ASSISTANCE. Selected students receive tuition, fees, books, laboratory expenses, and an allowance of $100 per month for up to ten months of each school year.

WHERE TO APPLY. Application information can be obtained from the professor of naval science (Navy ROTC) at the institution the student plans to enroll, or from:

NROTC
Commander, Navy Recruiting Command
4015 Wilson Boulevard
Arlington, Virginia 22203

Colleges and Universities participating in the Navy ROTC Scholarshp Program:

Auburn University
Auburn, Alabama 36830

California, University of
Berkeley, California 94720

California at Los Angeles, University of
Los Angeles, California 90024

Citadel, The
Charleston, South Carolina 29409

Colorado, University of
Boulder, Colorado 80302

Cornell University
Ithaca, New York 14850

Duke University
Durham, North Carolina 27706

Florida A and M University
Tallahassee, Florida 32307

Florida, University of
Gainesville, Florida 32601

Georgia Institute of Technology
Atlanta, Georgia 30332

Holy Cross, College of the
Worcester, Massachusetts 01610

Idaho, University of
Moscow, Idaho 83843

Illinois Institute of Technology
Chicago, Illinois 60616

Illinois, University of
Champaign, Illinois 61820

Iowa State University of Science and
    Technology
Ames, Iowa 50010

Jacksonville University
Jacksonville, Florida 32211

Kansas, University of
Lawrence, Kansas 66045

Louisville, University of
Louisville, Kentucky 40208

Maine Maritime Academy
Castine, Maine 04421

Marquette University
Milwaukee, Wisconsin 53233

Massachusetts Institute of Technology
Cambridge, Massachusetts 02139

Miami University
Oxford, Ohio 45056

Michigan, University of
Ann Arbor, Michigan 48104

Minnesota, University of
Minneapolis, Minnesota 55455

Mississippi, University of
University, Mississippi 38677

Missouri, University of
Columbia, Missouri 65201

Nebraska, University of
Lincoln, Nebraska 68505

New Mexico, University of
Albuquerque, New Mexico 87106

North Carolina, University of
Chapel Hill, North Carolina 27514

North Carolina Central University
Durham, North Carolina 27707

Northwestern University
Evanston, Illinois 60201

Notre Dame, University of
Notre Dame, Indiana 46556

Ohio State University
Columbus, Ohio 43210

Oklahoma, University of
Norman, Oklahoma 73069

Oregon State University
Corvallis, Oregon 97331

Pennsylvania State University
University Park, Pennsylvania 16802

Pennsylvania, University of
Philadelphia, Pennsylvania 19104

Prairie View A and M College
Prairie View, Texas 77445

Purdue University
West Lafayette, Indiana 47907

Rensselaer Polytechnic Institute
Troy, New York 12181

Rice University
Houston, Texas 77001

Rochester, University of
Rochester, New York 14627

Savannah State College
Savannah, Georgia 31404

South Carolina, University of
Columbia, South Carolina 29208

Southern California, University of
Los Angeles, California 90007

Southern University and A and M
   College
Baton Rouge, Louisiana 70813

Texas, University of
Austin, Texas 78712

Texas A and M University
College Station, Texas 77843

Tulane University of Louisiana
New Orleans, Louisiana 70118

Utah, University of
Salt Lake City, Utah 84112

Vanderbilt University
Nashville, Tennessee 37203

Villanova University
Villanova, Pennsylvania 19085

Virginia, University of
Charlottesville, Virginia 22903

Washington, University of
Seattle, Washington 98105

Wisconsin, University of
Madison, Wisconsin 53706

18. RESERVE OFFICER TRAINING CORPS SCHOLARSHIP PROGRAM (U. S. AIR FORCE)

PROVIDES four-year scholarship (plus monthly allowance) to a participating college or university.

ELIGIBILITY. Any student at least seventeen years of age who is acceptable for enrollment in one of the participating colleges or universities, is eligible for the competitive four-year scholarship, which will lead to a commission as second lieutenant in the U. S. Air Force. The student must be able to complete all requirements for a college degree and a commission prior to attaining age twenty-five.

(Three- and two-year scholarships are also available, but only to students already enrolled in Air Force ROTC.)

AMOUNT OF ASSISTANCE. Selected students receive tuition, fees, books, laboratory expenses, and a monthly allowance of $100 for the four-year program.

WHERE TO APPLY. Application information can be obtained from the professor of aerospace studies (U. S. Air Force ROTC) at the institution the student plans to enroll, or from:

Air Force ROTC
Directorate of Admissions
Maxwell Air Force Base, Alabama
   36112

Colleges and Universities participating in the Air Force ROTC Scholarship Program are listed below:

ALABAMA
   Alabama State University
   Montgomery 36101

   Auburn University
   Auburn 36830

   Livingston University
   Livingston 35470

   University of Alabama
   University 35486

   Samford University
   Birmingham 35209

   Troy State University
   Troy 36081

   Tuskegee Institute
   Tuskegee 36088

26

ARIZONA
Arizona State University
Tempe 85281

Northern Arizona University
Flagstaff 86001

University of Arizona
Tucson 85721

ARKANSAS
University of Arkansas
Fayetteville 72701

University of Arkansas
at Monticello
Monticello 71655

CALIFORNIA
Loyola University
of Los Angeles
Los Angeles 90045

University of California
at Berkeley
Berkeley 94720

University of California
at Los Angeles
Los Angeles 90024

University of Southern California
Los Angeles 90007

COLORADO
Colorado State University
Fort Collins 80521

University of Colorado
Boulder 80302

University of Northern Colorado
Greeley 80631

CONNECTICUT
University of Connecticut
Storrs 06268

DISTRICT OF COLUMBIA
Georgetown University
Washington, D.C. 20007

Howard University
Washington, D.C. 20001

FLORIDA
Embry-Riddle Aeronautical
University
Daytona Beach 32015

Florida State University
Tallahassee 32306

Florida Technological University
Orlando 32816

University of Florida
Gainesville 32601

University of Miami
Coral Gables 33124

GEORGIA
Emory University
Atlanta 30322

Georgia Institute of Technology
Atlanta 30332

University of Georgia
Athens 30601

Valdosta State College
Valdosta 31601

IDAHO
University of Idaho
Moscow 83843

ILLINOIS
Bradley University
Peoria 61606

Illinois Institute of Technology
Chicago 60616

Parks College
Cahokia 62206

Southern Illinois University
Carbondale 62901

Southern Illinois University
at Edwardsville
Edwardsville 62025

University of Illinois
Urbana 61801

INDIANA
Butler University
Indianapolis 46208

Indiana University
Bloomington 47401

Purdue University
Lafayette 47907

University of Evansville
Evansville 47701

University of Notre Dame
Notre Dame 46556

IOWA
Coe College
Cedar Rapids 52402

Drake University
Des Moines 50311

Iowa State University
Ames 50010

University of Iowa
Iowa City 52240

KANSAS
Kansas State University
Manhattan 66502

University of Kansas
Lawrence 66044

Washburn University
Topeka 66621

Wichita State University
Wichita 67208

KENTUCKY
University of Kentucky
Lexington 40506

University of Louisville
Louisville 40208

LOUISIANA
Grambling College
Grambling 71245

Louisiana Tech. University
Ruston 71270

Louisiana State University
and A and M College
Baton Rouge 70803

Nicholls State University
Thibodaux 70301

Tulane University
New Orleans 70118

University of Southwestern
Louisiana
Lafayette 70501

MAINE
Colby College
Waterville 04901

MARYLAND
University of Maryland
College Park 20742

University of Maryland,
Eastern Shore
Princess Anne 21853

MASSACHUSETTS
College of the Holy Cross
Worcester 01610

Lowell Technological Institute
Lowell 01854

Massachusetts Institute of Technology
Cambridge 02139

University of Massachusetts
Amherst 01002

MICHIGAN
Michigan State University
East Lansing 48823

University of Detroit
Detroit 48221

University of Michigan
Ann Arbor 48104

Michigan Technological University
Houghton 49931

MINNESOTA
St. Olaf College
Northfield 55057

The College of St. Thomas
St. Paul 55101

University of Minnesota
Minneapolis 55455

University of Minnesota at Duluth
Duluth 55812

MISSISSIPPI
Mississippi State University
State College 39762

Mississippi Valley State College
Itta Bena 38941

University of Mississippi
University 38677

University of Southern Mississippi
Hattiesburg 39401

MISSOURI
St. Louis University
St. Louis 63103

Southeast Missouri State College
Cape Girardeau 63701

University of Missouri
Columbia 65201

University of Missouri at Rolla
Rolla 65401

MONTANA
Montana State University
Bozeman 59715

University of Montana
Missoula 59801

NEBRASKA
University of Nebraska
Lincoln 68508

University of Nebraska at Omaha
Omaha 68101

NEW HAMPSHIRE
University of New Hampshire
Durham 03824

NEW JERSEY
Newark College of Engineering
Newark 07102

Rutgers, The State University
New Brunswick 08903

Stevens Institute of Technology
Hoboken 07030

NEW MEXICO
New Mexico State University
Las Cruces 88001

University of New Mexico
Albuquerque 87106

NEW YORK
Cornell University
Ithaca 14850

Fordham University
Bronx 10458

Manhattan College
Bronx 10471

Rensselaer Polytechnic Institute
Troy 12181

Syracuse University
Syracuse 13210

NORTH CAROLINA
Duke University
Durham 27706

East Carolina University
Greenville 27834

Fayetteville State University
Fayetteville 28301

North Carolina A and T State
  University
Greensboro 27411

North Carolina State University
  at Raleigh
Raleigh 27607

University of North Carolina
Chapel Hill 27514

NORTH DAKOTA
North Dakota State University
  of A and AS
Fargo 58102

University of North Dakota
Grand Forks 58201

OHIO
Bowling Green State University
Bowling Green 43402

Capital University
Columbus 43209

Denison University
Granville 43023

Kent State University
Kent 44240

Miami University
Oxford 45056

Ohio University
Athens 45701

Ohio State University
Columbus 43210

Ohio Wesleyan University
Delaware 43015

Otterbein College
Westerville 43081

The University of Akron
Akron 43304

University of Cincinnati
Cincinnati 45221

OKLAHOMA
Oklahoma State University
Stillwater 74074

The University of Oklahoma
Norman 73069

University of Tulsa
Tulsa 74104

OREGON
Oregon State University
Corvallis 97331

University of Oregon
Eugene 97403

University of Portland
Portland 97203

PENNSYLVANIA
Allegheny College
Meadville 16335

Duquesne University
Pittsburgh 15219

Grove City College
Grove City 16127

Lehigh University
Bethlehem 18015

The Pennsylvania State University
University Park 16802

University of Pittsburgh
Pittsburgh 15213

Wilkes College
Wilkes-Barre 18703

PUERTO RICO
College of Agriculture and
    Mechanic Arts
Mayaguez 00708

University of Puerto Rico
Rio Piedras 00931

SOUTH CAROLINA
Baptist College at Charleston
Charleston 29411

Clemson University
Clemson 29631

Newberry College
Newberry 29108

The Citadel
Charleston 29409

University of South Carolina
Columbia 29208

SOUTH DAKOTA
South Dakota State University
Brookings 57006

TENNESSEE
Memphis State University
Memphis 38111

Tennessee State University
Nashville 37203

University of Tennessee
Knoxville 37916

TEXAS
Angelo State University
San Angelo 76901

Baylor University
Waco 76703

East Texas State University
Commerce 75428

Lamar University
Beaumont 77710

North Texas State University
Denton 76203

Pan American University
Edinburg 78539

Southern Methodist University
Dallas 75222

Southwest Texas State University
San Marcos 78666

Sul Ross State University
Alpine 79830

Texas A and M University
College Station 77840

Texas Christian University
Fort Worth 76129

Texas Tech. University
Lubbock 79409

University of Texas at Austin
Austin 78712

UTAH
Brigham Young University
Provo 84601

Southern Utah State College
Cedar City 84720

Utah State University
Logan 84321

VERMONT
Norwich University
Northfield 05663

St. Michael's College
Winooski 05404

VIRGINIA
Virginia Military Institute
Lexington 24450

Virginia Polytechnic Institute
Blacksburg 24060

University of Virginia
Charlottesville 22903

WASHINGTON
University of Puget Sound
Tacoma 98416

University of Washington
Seattle 98105

Washington State University
Pullman 99163

WEST VIRGINIA
Davis and Elkins College
Elkins 26241

West Virginia University
Morgantown 26506

WISCONSIN
University of Wisconsin
at Madison
Madison 53706

University of Wisconsin
at Superior
Superior 54880

WYOMING
University of Wyoming
Laramie 82070

19. SOCIAL SECURITY CASH BENEFITS FOR STUDENTS

PROVIDES cash benefits for education of qualified students between eighteen and twenty-two years of age.

ELIGIBILITY. Student must be unmarried, between eighteen and twenty-two years old, and the dependent of a parent who receives Social Security disability or retirement benefits, or who is deceased and had worked under Social Security long enough to be insured. The recipient must be a full-time student at an accredited educational institution.

AMOUNT OF ASSISTANCE. Qualified students receive monthly cash benefits during the academic year and during vacation or other periods of nonattendance of up to four months (if full-time student prior to the nonattendance period and intends to resume attendance following this period).

Payment amounts vary, but the average monthly benefit is about $110 for a son or daughter of a deceased worker; somewhat less for a child of a retired or disabled worker.

WHERE TO APPLY. Students may apply for benefits or receive further information from any Social Security office.

20. HEALTH PROFESSIONS SCHOLARSHIP AND STUDENT LOAN PROGRAM

PROVIDES financial assistance in the form of scholarships and long-term, low-interest loans for qualified students.

SCHOLARSHIPS

ELIGIBILITY. Student must be a citizen or national of the United States or have such immigration status and personal plans to justify the conclusion that he intends to become a permanent resident of the United States. He must be in exceptional need of such assistance and must be enrolled and in good standing (or accepted for enrollment) as a full-time student pursuing a course of study leading to one of the following degrees:

bachelor of science in pharmacy or equivalent degree; doctor of medicine; doctor of dental surgery or equivalent degree; doctor of osteopathy; doctor of optometry or equivalent degree; doctor of podiatry or equivalent degree; or doctor of veterinary medicine or equivalent degree.

AMOUNT OF ASSISTANCE. Qualified students are awarded scholarships of up to $3,500 per year.

LOANS

ELIGIBILITY. Student must be a citizen or national of the United States or have such immigration status and personal plans to justify the conclusion that he intends to become a permanent resident of the United States. He must be enrolled (or accepted for enrollment) as a full-time student pursuing a course of study leading to one of the degrees listed above in the paragraph on scholarship eligibility. The student must also be in need of the loan to be able to pursue the course of study.

AMOUNT OF ASSISTANCE. Qualified students may borrow up to $3,500 per academic year at an interest rate of 3 percent. Repayment of loan is made over a ten-year period beginning one year after the student completes (or ceases to pursue) the prescribed course of study. Interest, at the rate of 3 percent per year on the unpaid balance, begins at the time the loan becomes repayable. Repayment of loan may be deferred or canceled under the following conditions:

1. *Deferred payment.* Repayment of principal may be deferred up to three years during periods of full-time active duty in the Army, Navy, Air Force, Marine Corps, Coast Guard, Coast and Geodetic Survey, or in the

Public Health Service, or a volunteer under the Peace Corps Act. If pursuing advanced professional training (including internships and residencies), repayment may be deferred up to five years for loans made before November 18, 1971, but after June 30, 1969. For loans made on or after November 18, 1971, there is no limitation on period of advanced professional training which may be deferred. Interest does not accrue during periods of deferment.

2. *Cancellation of loan.* If the borrower practices medicine, dentistry, osteopathy, optometry, pharmacy, podiatry, or veterinary medicine for at least two years in an area designated by the state health authority as having a shortage of, and need for, these professional services, the federal government will repay 60 percent of the outstanding principal and interest on such loans.

If the borrower should die or incur permanent and total disability, the unpaid balance of the loan (plus accrued interest) may be canceled.

WHERE TO APPLY. Application information may be obtained from the director of student financial aid at the school where the student intends to apply for admission, or from:

National Institutes of Health
Division of Physician and Health Professions Education
Bureau of Health Resources Development
Bethesda, Maryland 20014

A list of schools participating in the Health Professions Student Assistance Programs may be obtained from the above address.

21. **LAW ENFORCEMENT EDUCATION PROGRAM (LEEP)**

PROVIDES loans and grants to qualified students.

LOANS

ELIGIBILITY. To be eligible for a loan, the student must be enrolled (or accepted for enrollment) at a participating institution (designated by the Law Enforcement Assistance Administration) as a full-time student in a program of study directly related to law enforcement. The student must intend to pursue full-time employment in the criminal justice field upon completion of studies.

AMOUNT OF ASSISTANCE. Loans are made up to $2,200 per academic year to cover tuition, fees, and related expenses. If the borrower becomes a certified full-time employee of a public law enforcement agency, the loan is canceled at the rate of 25 percent per year of service in law enforcement. Otherwise, loans carry a 7 percent interest rate and are repayable within ten years or at the rate of $50 a month, whichever is the shorter time period.

GRANTS

ELIGIBILITY. To be eligible for a grant for tuition, the student must be a full-time employee of a publicly funded police or corrections agency, or the courts, and enrolled (or accepted for enrollment) on a full- or part-time basis in courses related to law enforcement at a participating institution designated by the Law Enforcement Assistance Administration.

AMOUNT OF ASSISTANCE. Grants are awarded to a maximum of $250 per quarter or $400 per semester. The grant recipient must agree to remain in full-time criminal justice employment for at least two years following completion of courses; otherwise, grants must be repayed.

WHERE TO APPLY. Application information may be obtained from the student financial aid officer of one of the participating institutions, or from:

Law Enforcement Assistance Administration
U. S. Department of Justice
Washington, D.C. 20530

22. INDIAN STUDENTS' SCHOLARSHIP AND LOAN PROGRAM

PROVIDES financial assistance in the form of scholarship grants and long-term, low-interest loans for needy and capable American Indians to attend a college or university of their choice.

SCHOLARSHIP GRANTS

ELIGIBILITY. Scholarship recipients must have one-quarter or more degree Indian, Eskimo, or Aleut blood of a tribal group served by the Bureau of Indian Affairs. Scholarships are made primarily to youth residing on Indian reservations or other Indian-owned, tax-exempt lands located nearby. Both financial need and scholastic ability are considered in determining the applicant's eligibility. (Since many colleges already have programs of financial aid applicable to Indian students, the applicant should seek such aid through the college of his or her choice before applying for federal scholarship assistance.)

AMOUNT OF ASSISTANCE. Selected qualified students may be awarded scholarships of various amounts dependent upon the individual's financial need. The average grant amount is about $1,300.

LOANS

ELIGIBILITY. Applicants must have one-quarter or more degree Indian blood, of tribes served by the Bureau of Indian Affairs, with preference given to those who live on Indian reservations or other Indian-owned, tax-exempt lands. Direct loans are made normally to applicants who are not eligible for loans from a corporation, tribe, or band conducting credit operations and who are ineligible for loans from a credit association.

AMOUNT OF ASSISTANCE. Qualified students may obtain educational loans of up to $500 for each school year from their respective area offices. Larger amounts are approved at the central office level.

WHERE TO APPLY. Application must be made (through the agency office having record of the applicant's tribal membership) to the appropriate area office. Agency and area offices are listed below. Application information may be obtained from the area director of the local agency of the Bureau of Indian Affairs, or from:

U. S. Department of the Interior
Bureau of Indian Affairs
Division of Student Services
123 4th Street, S.W.
P. O. Box 1788
Albuquerque, New Mexico 87103

Area and agency offices:

Aberdeen Area Office, 820 S. Main Street, Aberdeen, South Dakota 57401

Cheyenne River Agency,
Eagle Butte, South Dakota 57625

Fort Berthold Agency,
New Town, North Dakota 58763

Fort Totten Agency,
Fort Totten, North Dakota 58335

Pierre Agency,
Pierre, South Dakota 57501

Pine Ridge Agency,
Pine Ridge, South Dakota 57770

Rosebud Agency,
Rosebud, South Dakota 57570

Sisseton Agency,
Sisseton, South Dakota 57262

Standing Rock Agency,
Fort Yates, North Dakota 58538

Turtle Mountain Agency,
Belcourt, North Dakota 58316

Winnebago Agency,
Winnebago, Nebraska 68071

Yankton Agency,
Wagner, South Dakota 57380

Albuquerque Area Office, P. O. Box
8327, Albuquerque, New Mexico
87108

Consolidated Ute Agency,
P. O. Box 315,
Ignacio, Colorado 81137

Jicarilla Agency,
Dulce, New Mexico 87528

Mescalero Agency,
Mescalero, New Mexico 88340

Northern Pueblos Agency,
P. O. Box 580,
Santa Fe, New Mexico 87501

Southern Pueblos Agency,
P. O. Box 1667,
Albuquerque, New Mexico 87103

Zuni Agency,
Zuni, New Mexico 87327

Anadarko Area Office, Federal Building,
Anadarko, Oklahoma 73005

Anadarko Agency,
Anadarko, Oklahoma 73005

Concho Agency,
Concho, Oklahoma 73022

Horton Agency,
Horton, Kansas 66439

Pawnee Agency,
Pawnee, Oklahoma 74058

Shawnee Agency,
Shawnee, Oklahoma 74801

Billings Area Office, 316 N. 26th Street,
Billings, Montana 59101

Blackfeet Agency,
Browning, Montana 59417

Crow Agency,
Crow Agency, Montana 59022

Flathead Agency,
Ronan, Montana 59864

Fort Belknap Agency,
Harlem, Montana 59526

Fort Peck Agency,
P. O. Box 637,
Poplar, Montana 59255

Northern Cheyenne Agency,
Lame Deer, Montana 59043

Rocky Boy's Agency,
Box Elder, Montana 59521

Wind River Agency,
Fort Washakie, Wyoming 82514

Juneau Area Office, Box 3-8000,
Juneau, Alaska 99801

Anchorage District Office,
P. O. Box 120,
Anchorage, Alaska 99501

Bethel District Office,
P. O. Box 347,
Bethel, Alaska 99559

Fairbanks District Office,
P. O. Box 530,
Fairbanks, Alaska 99701

Nome District Office,
Nome, Alaska 99762

Southeast District Office,
P. O. Box 3-8000,
Juneau, Alaska 99801

Minneapolis Area Office, 831 Second Avenue South, Second Floor, Minneapolis, Minnesota 55402

Great Lakes Agency,
Ashland, Wisconsin 54806

Minnesota Agency,
Federal Building,
P. O. Box 489,
Bemidji, Minnesota 56601

Red Lake Agency,
Red Lake, Minnesota 56671

Sac and Fox Area Field Office,
Tama, Iowa 52339

Muskogee Area Office, Federal Building, Muskogee, Oklahoma 74401

Ardmore Agency,
P. O. Box 997,
Ardmore, Oklahoma 73401

Five Civilized Tribes Agency,
Federal Building,
Muskogee, Oklahoma 74401

Miami Agency,
P. O. Box 391,
Miami, Oklahoma 74354

Okmulgee Agency,
P. O. Box 671,
Okmulgee, Oklahoma 74447

Osage Agency,
Pawhuska, Oklahoma 74056

Tahlequah Agency,
P. O. Box 459,
Tahlequah, Oklahoma 74464

Talihina Agency,
P. O. Box 187,
Talihina, Oklahoma 74571

Wewoka Agency,
P. O. Box 1060,
Wewoka, Oklahoma 74884

Navajo Tribe, The, Division of Higher Education, Window Rock, Arizona 86515

Phoenix Area Office, P. O. Box 7007, Phoenix, Arizona 85011

Colorado River Agency,
Parker, Arizona 85344

Fort Apache Agency,
Whiteriver, Arizona 85941

Hopi Agency,
Keams Canyon, Arizona 86034

Nevada Agency,
Stewart, Nevada 89437

Papago Agency,
Sells, Arizona 85634

Pima Agency,
Sacaton, Arizona 85247

Salt River Agency,
Route 1,
Box 907,
Scottsdale, Arizona 85251

San Carlos Agency,
San Carlos, Arizona 85550

Truxton Canyon Agency,
Valentine, Arizona 86437

Uintah and Ouray Agency,
Fort Duchesne, Utah 84026

Portland Area Office, 1425 N.E. Irving Street, Box 3785, Portland, Oregon 97208

Colville Agency,
Coulee Dam, Washington 99116

Fort Hall Agency,
Fort Hall, Idaho 83203

Northern Idaho Agency,
Lapwai, Idaho 83540

Umatilla Agency,
Pendleton, Oregon 97801

Warm Springs Agency,
Warm Springs, Oregon 97761

Western Washington Agency,
3006 Colby Avenue,
Everett, Washington 98201

Yakima Agency,
Toppenish, Washington 98948

Sacramento Area Office, 2800 Cottage-
way, Sacramento, California 95825

California Agency,
P. O. Box 4775,
Sacramento, California 95825

Hoopa Area Field Office,
Hoopa, California 95546

Palm Springs Office,
587 S. Palm Canyon Drive,
Palm Springs, California 92262

Riverside Area Field Office,
6848 Magnolia Avenue, Suite 8,
Riverside, California 92506

Field Offices under Central Office, Washington, D.C. 20242

Cherokee Agency,
Cherokee, North Carolina 28719

Choctaw Agency,
Philadelphia, Mississippi 39350

Miccosukee Agency,
P. O. Box 1369,
Homestead, Florida 33030

New York Liaison Office,
Midtown Plaza,
700 East Water Street,
Syracuse, New York 13210

Seminole Agency,
6075 Stirling Road,
Hollywood, Florida 33024

Part II

SELECTED NONFEDERAL UNDERGRADUATE STUDENT ASSISTANCE PROGRAMS

1. NATIONAL MERIT SCHOLARSHIP PROGRAM

PROVIDES competitive four-year renewable Merit Scholarships as well as one-time nonrenewal National Merit $1,000 Scholarships.

ELIGIBILITY. A secondary student who wishes to compete for Merit Scholarships must take the Preliminary Scholastic Aptitude Test/National Merit Scholarship Qualifying Test (PSAT/NMSQT) in October of his junior year in high school. The student must be a U.S. citizen or plan to obtain U.S. citizenship, as soon as he is qualified to do so. In addition, he must plan to leave secondary school and enter college in the same calendar year, or plan to attend a regionally accredited U.S. college and to enroll in a course of study leading to one of the usual baccalaureate degrees.

AMOUNT OF ASSISTANCE. Winners of the National Merit $1,000 Scholarships each receive a one-time award of $1,000 after enrollment as full-time students in an accredited U.S. college or university in the fall term following their selection as a winner. Winners of the four-year Merit Scholarships receive scholarships that are renewable each year up to four years of full-time study or completion of undergraduate degree requirements, whichever comes first. The stipend that accompanies a four-year sponsored award may range from $100 to $1,500 per year and is based on the financial need of the scholarship winner.

WHERE TO APPLY. Taking the PSAT/NMSQT is a request for Merit Scholarship consideration, and further application to the National Merit Scholarship Corporation is not necessary. Students who wish to take the PSAT/NMSQT should register with their principal or counselor, from whom further information may be obtained.

2. NATIONAL ACHIEVEMENT SCHOLARSHIP PROGRAM (for outstanding black students)

PROVIDES competitive one-time nonrenewable National Achievement Scholarships as well as four-year renewable Achievement Scholarships for black students.

ELIGIBILITY. To participate in the Achievement Program, a black student must take the Preliminary Scholastic Aptitude Test/National Merit Scholarship Qualifying Test (PSAT/NMSQT) in his school and indicate in a space provided on the PSAT/NMSQT answer sheet that he is eligible and wishes to be considered in the Achievement Program as well as in the Merit Program. Other eligibility requirements are the same as those described for the preceding program (National Merit Scholarship Program).

AMOUNT OF ASSISTANCE. Winners of the one-time nonrenewable National Achievement $1,000 Scholarships receive a one-time award of $1,000 payable after his enrollment as a full-time student in a regionally accredited U.S. college or university in the fall term following his selection as a winner. There is no restriction on the winner's college choice, course of study, or career choice.

Winners of the four-year sponsored Achievement Scholarships receive scholarships that are renewable each year up to four years of full-time study or completion of undergraduate degree requirements, whichever is earlier. Four-year Achievement Scholarship winners also receive for each year of college a stipend that ranges from a minimum of $250 per year to a maximum of $1,500 per year.

WHERE TO APPLY.   Taking the PSAT/ NMSQT and marking the Achievement Program grid constitute a request for consideration for Achievement Scholarship, and no other application is necessary. Students who wish to take the PSAT/NMSQT should register with their principal or counselor, from whom further information may be obtained.

3. NATIONAL SCHOLARSHIP SERVICE AND FUND FOR NEGRO STUDENTS (NSSFNS)

PROVIDES a free computerized college advisory and referral service for black high school students interested in continuing their education, and limited supplementary scholarship aid for qualified students who have been counseled by NSSFNS.

ELIGIBILITY.   Black high school students (juniors and seniors) and all Upward Bound and Talent Search students who desire to obtain admission to a post-secondary institution are eligible to apply. There are no minimum test scores or grade average requirements or fees for applicants.

AMOUNT OF ASSISTANCE.   Students receive referrals to several institutions which should be able to provide admission and financial aid. General information about application procedures and financial aid resources is also provided. In addition, a student who has been counseled by the NSSFNS college advisory and referral service is eligible to apply for a supplementary scholarship (which ranges from $200 to $600 per year and is renewable through the junior

year in college) if he meets the following criteria:

1. the student has been admitted to a two- or four-year college.
2. the student has received from the college, or another source, a scholarship of $200 or more.
3. the student has insufficient funds to meet the total yearly college costs even after all other sources of aid have been exhausted.

WHERE TO APPLY.   Applications may be obtained from the high school guidance counselor or by writing directly to:

National Scholarship Service and Fund
  for Negro Students
1776 Broadway
New York, New York 10019

4. UNITED PRESBYTERIAN CHURCH, U.S.A. SCHOLARSHIP AND EDUCATIONAL LOAN PROGRAM

PROVIDES scholarships and long-term, low-interest loans for students who qualify in any of several programs.

NATIONAL PRESBYTERIAN COLLEGE SCHOLARSHIPS

ELIGIBILITY.   To be considered for these scholarships a student must be a communicant member of the United Presbyterian Church, U.S.A. Students must be able to complete secondary school and enter one of the colleges related to the Board of Christian Education of the United Presbyterian Church, U.S.A., in the same calendar year. A student's scholastic record, his score in the Scholastic Aptitude Test, and his personal qualities are also factors in distribution of the scholarships.

AMOUNT OF ASSISTANCE. Awards range from $100 to $1,400 according to a student's need.

WHERE TO APPLY. Application information may be obtained by writing to:

National Presbyterian College Scholarships
FINANCIAL AID FOR STUDIES
United Presbyterian Church in the U.S.A.
475 Riverside Drive
New York, New York 10027

EDUCATIONAL ASSISTANCE PROGRAM (EAP)

ELIGIBILITY. Only children of full-time trained religious leaders employed by a church or a judicatory (for example, a presbytery) of the United Presbyterian Church, U.S.A. may qualify for this program. In addition, the student must be attending or planning to attend an accredited college, university, or vocational school on a full-time basis.

AMOUNT OF ASSISTANCE. Awards range from $400 to $1,400 according to a student's need as determined by the College Scholarship Service, and by resources available to the EAP.

WHERE TO APPLY. Application information may be obtained by writing to:

Educational Assistance Program
FINANCIAL AID FOR STUDIES
United Presbyterian Church in the U.S.A.
475 Riverside Drive
New York, New York 10027

SAMUEL ROBINSON SCHOLARSHIPS (WESTMINSTER SHORTER CATECHISM SCHOLARSHIPS)

ELIGIBILITY. A student must be an undergraduate in a United Presbyterian college. In addition, the student must successfully recite the 107 answers of the Westminster Shorter Catechism and write a 2,000-word essay on an assigned topic related to the Shorter Catechism. The essay and the college's certification of the student's recitation should be sent to the Office of Educational Loans and Scholarships before a specified date.

AMOUNT OF ASSISTANCE. Winners of the scholarship competition each receive an award of $300.

WHERE TO APPLY. Application information (including the essay topic) may be obtained by asking the head of the Religion Department of the United Presbyterian college, or by writing to:

Samuel Robinson Scholarships
Manager, FINANCIAL AID FOR STUDIES
Vocation Agency, UPCUSA
475 Riverside Drive
New York, New York 10027

STUDENT OPPORTUNITY SCHOLARSHIPS

ELIGIBILITY. Young persons of limited opportunities, particularly from ethnic minority groups, who are enrolled (or accepted for enrollment) in a college and who would be unable to receive higher education without financial aid, are eligible.

AMOUNT OF ASSISTANCE. The amount of the scholarship varies according to a student's need as determined by the College Scholarship Service. Maximum grant is $1,200.

WHERE TO APPLY. Application information may be obtained by writing to:

Student Opportunity Scholarships
FINANCIAL AID FOR STUDIES
United Presbyterian Church in the U.S.A.
475 Riverside Drive
New York, New York 10027

STUDENT LOAN FUND

ELIGIBILITY. Students must be members of the United Presbyterian Church, U.S.A., be citizens of the United States, be registered with or under care of a presbytery or preparing for service in a denominational board, or already be in a church occupation. Students may be undergraduates in the junior or senior year, theological students, or graduate or professional students.

AMOUNT OF ASSISTANCE. A student may borrow up to $1,500 per academic year and $500 for summer school. Loans (plus 3 percent interest) are repayable monthly over a six-year period beginning six months after the student completes or ceases to pursue full-time study.

WHERE TO APPLY. Application information may be obtained by writing to:

Student Loan Fund
FINANCIAL AID FOR STUDIES
United Presbyterian Church in the U.S.A.
475 Riverside Drive
New York, New York 10027

5. AMERICAN BAPTIST STUDENT AID PROGRAM

PROVIDES students who qualify with long-term loans.

ELIGIBILITY. Any American Baptist student who is a citizen of the United States and is enrolled (or accepted for enrollment) as a full-time degree candidate in an accredited U.S. institution of higher education is eligible providing he shows need of financial assistance.

AMOUNT OF ASSISTANCE. An undergraduate student may borrow up to $500 per academic year with a maximum total of $2,000 over a four-year period. (A graduate or seminary student may borrow up to $1,000 per academic year with a maximum total of $3,000 over a three-year period.) A promissory note must be signed by the student and endorsed by another responsible person. Loans are repayable over a six-year period beginning the January after graduation or at the end of full-time study, with interest rates of 10 percent the first two years, 15 percent the third and fourth years, and 25 percent for the fifth and sixth years.

WHERE TO APPLY. Application information is available by writing to:

American Baptist Student Aid Fund
American Baptist Board of Education and Publication
Valley Forge, Pennsylvania 19481

6. UNITED METHODIST SCHOLARSHIP PROGRAM AND LOAN FUND

PROVIDES scholarships and long-term, low-interest loans for qualified students.

SCHOLARSHIPS

ELIGIBILITY. Students must be members of the United Methodist Church for at least one year and enrolled (or accepted for enrollment) as a full-time degree candidate in an accredited university, college, or junior college related to the United Methodist Church. If applying for a scholarship as a freshman, the student must have been in the upper 20 percent of his high school graduating class. If already in college, he must be in the upper third of his undergraduate class. Additional requirements are that the student be active in church programs and that he demonstrate outstanding personal qualities.

AMOUNT OF ASSISTANCE. A student may be awarded a scholarship of $500 per year for two of his four years in college.

WHERE TO APPLY. Application forms may be obtained from the United Methodist Scholarship officer of the accredited United Methodist school the student plans to enter. Completed forms along with a certificate of church membership, a high school recommendation (if an incoming freshman), and a one hundred-word essay, "Contributions I Am Making to the Religious Life of My Community," are to be returned to the United Methodist Scholarship officer. The scholarship committee of the college reviews the applications and sends recommendations to the Board of Higher Education and Ministry of the United Methodist Church in Nashville, which makes the final decisions concerning the awards.

The United Methodist colleges and universities participating in the program are:

Adrian College
Alaska Methodist University
Albion College
Albright College
Allegheny College
American University
Andrew College
Athens College
Baker University
Baldwin-Wallace College
Bennett College
Bethune-Cookman College
Birmingham-Southern College
Boston University
Brevard College
Centenary College for Women

Centenary College of Louisiana
Central Methodist College
Claflin College
Clark College
Columbia College
Cornell College
Dakota Wesleyan University
DePauw University
Dickinson College
Dillard University
Drew University
Duke University
Emory and Henry College
Emory University
Ferrum Junior College
Florida Southern College
Green Mountain College
Greensboro College
Hamline University
Hawaii Loa College
Hendrix College
High Point College
Hiwassee College
Huntingdon College
Huston-Tillotson College
Illinois Wesleyan University
Indiana Central College
Iowa Wesleyan College
Kansas Wesleyan
Kendall College
Kentucky Wesleyan College
LaGrange College
Lambuth College
Lawrence University
Lebanon Valley College
Lindsey Wilson College
Lon Morris College
Louisburg College
Lycoming College
MacMurray College

Martin College
McKendree College
McMurry College
Meharry Medical College
Methodist College
Millsaps College
Morningside College
Morristown College
Mount Union College
Nebraska Wesleyan University
North Carolina Wesleyan College
North Central College
Northwestern University
Ohio Northern University
Ohio Wesleyan University
Otterbein College
Oxford College of Emory University
Paine College
Pfeiffer College
Philander Smith College
Randolph-Macon College
Randolph-Macon Woman's College
Reinhardt College
Rocky Mountain College
Rust College
Scarritt College
Shenandoah College
Simpson College
Southern Methodist University
Southwestern College
Southwestern University
Spartanburg Junior College
Sue Bennett College
Syracuse University
Tennessee Wesleyan College
Texas Wesleyan College
Union College
University of Denver
University of Evansville
University of Puget Sound

University of the Pacific
Virginia Wesleyan College
Wesley College
Wesleyan College
West Virginia Wesleyan College
Western Maryland College
Westmar College
Westminster College
Wiley College
Willamette University
Wofford College
Wood Junior College
Young Harris College

LOANS

ELIGIBILITY. Students must be members of the United Methodist Church and enrolled full-time in a degree program in an accredited college in the United States. The student must be attending the college before he applies for the loan. Applicants must maintain a "C" average by the end of their second semester to receive further loans.

AMOUNT OF ASSISTANCE. Qualified students may borrow from $500 to $750 per academic year, depending on their student classification (freshman to graduate), with a maximum total of $4,000. Students in accredited junior colleges other than United Methodist schools may borrow up to $250 per academic year. A promissory note must be signed by the student and endorsed by a responsible person. Loans (plus 3 percent interest) are payable over a six-year period beginning six months after the student ceases to pursue full-time study.

WHERE TO APPLY. Application forms may be obtained from the loan officer of the college the student attends. The name of the loan officer at a United Methodist college or university can be obtained from the dean's office. At state and independent colleges and universities, the United Methodist minister to students ordinarily serves as loan officer for the United Methodist Student Loan Fund. The name of the loan officer at other private and professional schools may be obtained by writing to:

Section of Loans and Scholarships
Board of Higher Education and Ministry
The United Methodist Church, P. O.
    Box 871
Nashville, Tennessee 37202

7. KNIGHTS OF COLUMBUS SCHOLARSHIP PROGRAM

PROVIDES scholarships for undergraduate studies (in a Catholic institution) leading to a bachelor's degree.

ELIGIBILITY. Recipient must be a member of the Knights of Columbus, or a son or daughter of a member or deceased member. Scholarships are competitive and are awarded on the basis of academic excellence.

AMOUNT OF ASSISTANCE. Recipients receive scholarships of $1,000 per year, are renewable each year up to four years subject to satisfactory academic performance.

WHERE TO APPLY. Application information may be obtained by writing to:

Director of Scholarship Aid
Knights of Columbus, Supreme Council
Columbus Plaza
P. O. Drawer 1670
New Haven, Connecticut 06507

8. AID ASSOCIATION FOR LUTHERANS SCHOLARSHIP PROGRAMS

AAL ALL-COLLEGE SCHOLARSHIP PROGRAM

PROVIDES financial assistance for students to pursue college degrees.

ELIGIBILITY. Student must be a graduating high school senior planning to enroll at any Lutheran or other accredited college or university, with grades that meet entrance standards of the college or university. In addition, the student must hold an Aid Association for Lutherans life or health insurance certificate in his or her own name.

AMOUNT OF ASSISTANCE. Scholarship awards range from $200 to $1,750 per year, depending on the financial need of the individual. These scholarships are renewable for three additional years.

WHERE TO APPLY. Application information may be obtained by writing to:

AAL All-College Scholarship Program
Educational Testing Service
Box 176
Princeton, New Jersey 08540

AAL LUTHERAN CAMPUS SCHOLARSHIP PROGRAM

PROVIDES scholarships to Lutheran-owned and -operated and Lutheran Church-affiliated colleges, universities, and seminaries.

ELIGIBILITY. The student must be enrolled (or accepted for enrollment) in one of the sixty-three participating Lutheran colleges, universities, and seminaries. Scholarship grants are based on academic achievement, financial need, and other factors as determined by the Scholarship Selection Committee.

AMOUNT OF ASSISTANCE. Scholarship amounts vary and are determined by the Scholarship Selection Committee at each school.

WHERE TO APPLY. Application information may be obtained from the financial aid office of the school in which the student is enrolled or planning to enroll.

Participating Lutheran colleges, universities, and seminaries are as follows:

Alabama Lutheran Academy and College
Selma, Alabama 36701

Augsburg College
Minneapolis, Minnesota 55404

Augustana College
Rock Island, Illinois 61201

Augustana College
Sioux Falls, South Dakota 57102

Bethany College
Lindsborg, Kansas 67456

Bethany Lutheran College and Seminary
Mankato, Minnesota 56001

California Lutheran Bible School
Los Angeles, California 90006

California Lutheran College
Thousand Oaks, California 91360

Capital University
Columbus, Ohio 43209

Carthage College
Kenosha, Wisconsin 53140

Concordia College
Bronxville, New York 10708

Concordia College
Milwaukee, Wisconsin 53208

Concordia College
Moorhead, Minnesota 56560

Concordia College
Portland, Oregon 97211

Concordia College
St. Paul, Minnesota 55104

Concordia Lutheran Junior College
Ann Arbor, Michigan 48105

Concordia Lutheran College
Austin, Texas 78705

Concordia Senior College
Fort Wayne, Indiana 46805

Concordia Teachers College
River Forest, Illinois 60305

Concordia Teachers College
Seward, Nebraska 68435

Dana College
Blair, Nebraska 68008

Dr. Martin Luther College
New Ulm, Minnesota 56073

Gettysburg College
Gettysburg, Pennsylvania 17325

Golden Valley Lutheran College
Minneapolis, Minnesota 55422

Grand View College
Des Moines, Iowa 50316

Gustavus Adolphus College
St. Peter, Minnesota 56082

Lenoir Rhyne College
Hickory, North Carolina 28601

Luther College
Decorah, Iowa 52101

Luther College of the Bible and Liberal Arts
Teaneck, New Jersey 07666

Lutheran Bible Institute
Seattle, Washington 98133

Lutheran Deaconess Association
Valparaiso, Indiana 46383

Midland Lutheran College
Fremont, Nebraska 68025

Muhlenberg College
Allentown, Pennsylvania 18104

Newberry College
Newberry, South Carolina 29108

Northwestern College
Watertown, Wisconsin 53094

Pacific Lutheran University
Tacoma, Washington 98447

Roanoke College
Salem, Virginia 24153

St. John's College
Winfield, Kansas 67156

St. Olaf College
Northfield, Minnesota 55057

St. Paul's College
Concordia, Missouri 64020

Suomi College
Hancock, Michigan 49930

Susquehanna University
Selinsgrove, Pennsylvania 17870

Texas Lutheran College
Seguin, Texas 78155

Thiel College
Greenville, Pennsylvania 16125

Upsala College
East Orange, New Jersey 07019

Valparaiso University
Valparaiso, Indiana 46383

Wagner College
Staten Island, New York 10301

Waldorf College
Forest City, Iowa 50436

Wartburg College
Waverly, Iowa 50677

Wittenberg University
Springfield, Ohio 45501

Seminaries

Concordia Seminary
St. Louis, Missouri 63105

Concordia Theological Seminary
Springfield, Illinois 62702

Evangelical Lutheran Theological Seminary, The
Columbus, Ohio 43209

Hamma School of Theology
Springfield, Ohio 45501

Luther Theological Seminary
St. Paul, Minnesota 55108

Lutheran School of Theology at Chicago
Chicago, Illinois 60615

Lutheran Theological Seminary
Gettysburg, Pennsylvania 17325

Lutheran Theological Seminary at Philadelphia, The
Philadelphia, Pennsylvania 19119

Lutheran Theological Southern Seminary
Columbia, South Carolina 29203

Northwestern Lutheran Theological Seminary
St. Paul, Minnesota 55108

Pacific Lutheran Theological Seminary
Berkeley, California 94708

Wartburg Theological Seminary
Dubuque, Iowa 52001

Wisconsin Lutheran Seminary
Mequon, Wisconsin 53092

9. AMVETS MEMORIAL SCHOLARSHIP PROGRAM

PROVIDES scholarship grants for undergraduate college study.

ELIGIBILITY. Any high school senior whose father (or mother) is deceased and a veteran of World War II, or the Korean Conflict, or the Vietnam era is eligible for this scholarship grant. Also eligible is any high school senior whose father (or mother) is totally disabled as a result of military service during World

49

War II, the Korean Conflict, or the Vietnam era. Priority is awarded candidates whose fathers or mothers are totally disabled as a result of military service.

AMOUNT OF ASSISTANCE. Scholarship grants range from a minimum of $500 to a maximum of $1,000 for four years and may be used at any accredited college of the student's choice.

WHERE TO APPLY. Application information may be obtained from any AMVET post, national service officer, or by writing to:

AMVETS National Scholarship Program
1710 Rhode Island Avenue, N.W.
Washington, D.C. 20036

mended by club officials. Scholarships are competitive.

AMOUNT OF ASSISTANCE. Scholarships are outright grants that cover tuition and housing at twelve universities where the Evans Scholars Chapter Houses are maintained by the Foundation. They include the University of Colorado, the University of Illinois, Indiana University, Marquette University, the University of Michigan, Michigan State University, the University of Minnesota, the University of Missouri, Northwestern University, Ohio State University, Purdue University, and the University of Wisconsin. In other states, scholarships cover tuition and room-rent costs at the candidate's state university.

WHERE TO APPLY. Application information may be obtained by writing to:

Western Golf Association
Gold, Illinois 60029

10. EVANS SCHOLARS FOUNDATION SCHOLARSHIP PROGRAM

PROVIDES scholarships that are renewable for four years.

ELIGIBILITY. The student must have completed his junior year in high school and rank in the upper 25 percent of his class. He must have outstanding personal character, require financial assistance in order to attend college, and have a superior caddie record for a minimum of two years. In addition, he must be recom-

11. GENERAL MOTORS SCHOLARSHIP PLAN

PROVIDES four-year scholarship awards.

ELIGIBILITY. Any secondary school senior or graduate who is a citizen of the United States is eligible for consideration for a General Motors scholarship.

AMOUNT OF ASSISTANCE. Scholarship awards range from $200 to a maximum of $2,000 per year, depending upon demonstrated need.

WHERE TO APPLY. Application information may be obtained by writing to the director of admissions of one of the participating colleges and universities.

50

PARTICIPATING COLLEGES AND UNIVERSITIES ARE AS FOLLOWS:

(Institutions participate on an alternating-year basis. Those colleges participating 1973–74 and every other year thereafter are listed below as are also those colleges participating in 1974–75 and every other year thereafter.)

Colleges and universities participating in 1974–75 and every year thereafter.

University of Alabama
University, Alabama

Albion College
Albion, Michigan

Alma College
Alma, Michigan

University of Arizona
Tucson, Arizona

Auburn University
Auburn, Alabama

Ball State University
Muncie, Indiana

Boston College
Chestnut Hill, Massachusetts

Bowling Green State University
Bowling Green, Ohio

Butler University
Indianapolis, Indiana

California Institute of Technology
Pasadena, California

University of California, Berkeley
Berkeley, California

University of California, Los Angeles
Los Angeles, California

Canisius College
Buffalo, New York

Carnegie-Mellon University
Pittsburgh, Pennsylvania

Case Western Reserve University
Cleveland, Ohio

Central Michigan University
Mount Pleasant, Michigan

University of Chicago
Chicago, Illinois

University of Cincinnati
Cincinnati, Ohio

Clarkson College of Technology
Potsdam, New York

Cleveland State University
Cleveland, Ohio

University of Colorado
Boulder, Colorado

Columbia University
New York, New York

Cornell University
Ithaca, New York

Dartmouth College
Hanover, New Hampshire

University of Dayton
Dayton, Ohio

University of Delaware
Newark, Delaware

University of Denver
Denver, Colorado

Detroit Institute of Technology
Detroit, Michigan

University of Detroit
Detroit, Michigan

Drexel University
Philadelphia, Pennsylvania

Duke University
Durham, North Carolina

Duquesne University
Pittsburgh, Pennsylvania

Eastern Michigan University
Ypsilanti, Michigan

51

Ferris State College
Big Rapids, Michigan

Flint College
Flint, Michigan

University of Florida
Gainesville, Florida

Fordham University
New York, New York

Georgia Institute of Technology
Atlanta, Georgia

University of Georgia
Athens, Georgia

Hampton Institute
Hampton, Virginia

Harvard University
Cambridge, Massachusetts

Hillsdale College
Hillsdale, Michigan

College of the Holy Cross
Worcester, Massachusetts

Illinois Institute of Technology
Chicago, Illinois

University of Illinois
Urbana, Illinois

Indiana University
Bloomington, Indiana

Iowa State University of Science and
   Technology
Ames, Iowa

University of Iowa
Iowa City, Iowa

John Carroll University
Cleveland, Ohio

Kansas State University
Manhattan, Kansas

University of Kansas
Lawrence, Kansas

Kent State University
Kent, Ohio

Lawrence Institute of Technology
Southfield, Michigan

Lehigh University
Bethlehem, Pennsylvania

Loyola University of Chicago
Chicago, Illinois

Marquette University
Milwaukee, Wisconsin

Massachusetts Institute of Technology
Cambridge, Massachusetts

Miami University
Oxford, Ohio

University of Miami
Coral Gables, Florida

Michigan State University
East Lansing, Michigan

Michigan Technological University
Houghton, Michigan

University of Michigan
Ann Arbor, Michigan

University of Minnesota
Minneapolis, Minnesota

Mississippi State University
State College, Mississippi

University of Missouri
Columbia, Missouri

University of Missouri at Rolla
Rolla, Missouri

University of Nebraska
Lincoln, Nebraska

University of New Mexico
Albuquerque, New Mexico

New York University
New York, New York

State University of New York at Buffalo
Buffalo, New York

Niagara University
Niagara University, New York

North Carolina A&T State University
Greensboro, North Carolina

University of North Carolina
Chapel Hill, North Carolina

North Carolina State University at
   Raleigh
Raleigh, North Carolina

University of North Dakota
Grand Forks, North Dakota

Northeastern University
Boston, Massachusetts

Northwestern University
Evanston, Illinois

University of Notre Dame
Notre Dame, Indiana

Oakland University
Rochester, Michigan

Ohio State University
Columbus, Ohio

Ohio University
Athens, Ohio

Oklahoma City University
Oklahoma City, Oklahoma

Oklahoma State University
Stillwater, Oklahoma

University of Oklahoma
Norman, Oklahoma

University of Oregon
Eugene, Oregon

The Pennsylvania State University
University Park, Pennsylvania

University of Pennsylvania
Philadelphia, Pennsylvania

University of Pittsburgh
Pittsburgh, Pennsylvania

Princeton University
Princeton, New Jersey

Purdue University
West Lafayette, Indiana

Rensselaer Polytechnic Institute
Troy, New York

University of Rochester
Rochester, New York

Rochester Institute of Technology
Rochester, New York

Rose-Hulman Institute of Technology
Terre Haute, Indiana

St. Louis University
St. Louis, Missouri

South Dakota State University
Brookings, South Dakota

University of Southern California
Los Angeles, California

Southern Methodist University
Dallas, Texas

Stanford University
Stanford, California

Syracuse University
Syracuse, New York

Temple University
Philadelphia, Pennsylvania

Tennessee State University
Nashville, Tennessee

University of Tennessee
Knoxville, Tennessee

Texas A&M University
College Station, Texas

Texas Christian University
Fort Worth, Texas

University of Texas
Austin, Texas

University of Toledo
Toledo, Ohio

Tri-State College
Angola, Indiana

Tuskegee Institute
Tuskegee Institute, Alabama

University of Utah
Salt Lake City, Utah

Valparaiso University
Valparaiso, Indiana

Vanderbilt University
Nashville, Tennessee

Villanova University
Villanova, Pennsylvania

Virginia Polytechnic Institute and State
   University
Blacksburg, Virginia

Washington University
St. Louis, Missouri

Wayne State University
Detroit, Michigan

Western Michigan University
Kalamazoo, Michigan

West Virginia University
Morgantown, West Virginia

Wilberforce University
Wilberforce, Ohio

University of Wisconsin
Madison, Wisconsin

Worcester Polytechnic Institute
Worcester, Massachusetts

Xavier University
Cincinnati, Ohio

Yale University
New Haven, Connecticut

Youngstown State University
Youngstown, Ohio

**Colleges and universities participating in
1973–74 and every other year thereafter.**

Adrian College
Adrian, Michigan

University of Akron
Akron, Ohio

Anderson College
Anderson, Indiana

Aquinas College
Grand Rapids, Michigan

Arizona State University
Tempe, Arizona

University of Arkansas
Fayetteville, Arkansas

Baldwin-Wallace College
Berea, Ohio

Ball State University
Muncie, Indiana

Berea College
Berea, Kentucky

Boston University
Boston, Massachusetts

Bradley University
Peoria, Illinois

Brown University
Providence, Rhode Island

Bucknell University
Lewisburg, Pennsylvania

Butler University
Indianapolis, Indiana

California Institute of Technology
Pasadena, California

University of California, Berkeley
Berkeley, California

Case Western Reserve University
Cleveland, Ohio

Central Missouri State College
Warrensburg, Missouri

University of Cincinnati
Cincinnati, Ohio

City College of New York
New York, New York

Clarkson College of Technology
Potsdam, New York

Colgate University
Hamilton, New York

Columbia University
New York, New York

Cornell University
Ithaca, New York

Dartmouth College
Hanover, New Hampshire

University of Dayton
Dayton, Ohio

DePauw University
Greencastle, Indiana

University of Detroit
Detroit, Michigan

Drake University
Des Moines, Iowa

Emory University
Atlanta, Georgia

Fairleigh Dickinson University
Rutherford, New Jersey

Fordham University
New York, New York

Franklin College
Franklin, Indiana

Furman University
Greenville, South Carolina

George Washington University
Washington, D.C.

Georgetown University
Washington, D.C.

Georgia Institute of Technology
Atlanta, Georgia

University of Georgia
Athens, Georgia

Harvard University
Cambridge, Massachusetts

Illinois Institute of Technology
Chicago, Illinois

University of Illinois
Urbana, Illinois

Indiana Institute of Technology
Fort Wayne, Indiana

Indiana State University
Terre Haute, Indiana

Indiana University
Bloomington, Indiana

Iona College
New Rochelle, New York

Iowa State University
Ames, Iowa

University of Iowa
Iowa City, Iowa

Johns Hopkins University
Baltimore, Maryland

Kalamazoo College
Kalamazoo, Michigan

Kansas State University
Manhattan, Kansas

University of Kansas
Lawrence, Michigan

University of Kentucky
Lexington, Kentucky

Lafayette College
Easton, Pennsylvania

Lawrence Institute of Technology
Southfield, Michigan

Lehigh University
Bethlehem, Pennsylvania

Loyola College
Baltimore, Maryland

Louisiana State University
Baton Rouge, Louisiana

University of Maine
Orono, Maine

Manhattan College
New York, New York

Marquette University
Milwaukee, Wisconsin

Marygrove College
Detroit, Michigan

University of Maryland
College Park, Maryland

Massachusetts Institute of Technology
Cambridge, Massachusetts

Miami University
Oxford, Ohio

Michigan State University
East Lansing, Michigan

Michigan Technological University
Houghton, Michigan

University of Michigan
Ann Arbor, Michigan

Millikin University
Decatur, Illinois

University of Minnesota
Minneapolis, Minnesota

University of Missouri—Columbia
Columbia, Missouri

University of Missouri—Kansas City
Kansas City, Missouri

University of Missouri—Rolla
Rolla, Missouri

University of Nebraska
Lincoln, Nebraska

Newark College of Engineering
Newark, New Jersey

New York University
New York, New York

North Dakota State University
Fargo, North Dakota

North Texas State University
Denton, Texas

Northern Michigan University
Marquette, Michigan

Northwestern University
Evanston, Illinois

University of Notre Dame
Notre Dame, Indiana

Ohio State University
Columbus, Ohio

Ohio University
Athens, Ohio

Ohio Wesleyan University
Delaware, Ohio

Olivet College
Olivet, Michigan

Oregon State University
Corvallis, Oregon

Otterbein College
Westerville, Ohio

Pace College
New York, New York

Pennsylvania State University
University Park, Pennsylvania

University of Pennsylvania
Philadelphia, Pennsylvania

University of Pittsburgh
Pittsburgh, Pennsylvania

Princeton University
Princeton, New Jersey

Purdue University
Lafayette, Indiana

Rensselaer Polytechnic Institute
Troy, New York

Rider College
Trenton, New Jersey

University of Rochester
Rochester, New York

Rockhurst College
Kansas City, Missouri

Rose-Hulman Institute of Technology
Terre Haute, Indiana

Rutgers, The State University
New Brunswick, New Jersey

St. Bonaventure University
St. Bonaventure, New York

St. Francis College
Loretto, Pennsylvania

St. John's University
Jamaica, New York

St. Lawrence University
Canton, New York

St. Louis University
St. Louis, Missouri

San Jose State College
San Jose, California

Seton Hall University
South Orange, New Jersey

University of South Carolina
Columbia, South Carolina

South Dakota School of Mines and
  Technology
Rapid City, South Dakota

Southern Illinois University
Carbondale, Illinois

Stanford University
Stanford, California

Stevens Institute of Technology
Hoboken, New Jersey

Stout State University
Menomonie, Wisconsin

Syracuse University
Syracuse, New York

Tri-State College
Angola, Indiana

Tufts University
Medford, Massachusetts

University of Vermont
Burlington, Vermont

University of Virginia
Charlottesville, Virginia

Wabash College
Crawfordsville, Indiana

University of Washington
Seattle, Washington

Wayne State University
Detroit, Michigan

Western Michigan University
Kalamazoo, Michigan

University of Wisconsin
Madison, Wisconsin

Wittenberg University
Springfield, Ohio

Yale University
New Haven, Connecticut

12. PICKETT & HATCHER EDUCATIONAL LOAN PROGRAM

PROVIDES loans to qualified students for college education.

ELIGIBILITY. Students who are citizens of the United States and who would be unable to complete an education without financial assistance are eligible. Other factors considered include scholastic achievement and moral responsibility.

AMOUNT OF ASSISTANCE. Students may borrow up to $1,200 per school (or academic) year based on the amount required for fees, tuition, and room and board. Students may borrow additional amounts when they are attending summer school, or if they are attending on a year-round basis, up to a maximum of $4,800. Loans will bear interest of 2 percent per annum during the time the borrower remains in college and 6 percent per annum upon graduation or leaving college for a period in excess of six months. Repayment of loans plus 6 percent interest will begin six months after a borrower leaves his college or university. Payments of not less than 10 percent of the income of the recipient— or not less than one twelfth of 10 percent of the total amount borrowed (whichever may be larger)—will be made in equal monthly payments.

WHERE TO APPLY. Application information may be obtained by writing to:

Pickett & Hatcher Educational Fund
P. O. Box 2128
Columbus, Georgia 31902

13. JOURNALISM SCHOLARSHIP AND LOAN PROGRAM

PROVIDES financial aid for students who want to study journalism.

ELIGIBILITY. Any student wishing to study journalism is eligible for a grant or a loan to pursue college studies. Eligibility is based on various factors such as scholarship, need, interest, and ability, as specified by the source of the scholarship or loan.

AMOUNT OF ASSISTANCE. Over three thousand scholarship grants and over $4 million in loan programs are available in varying amounts.

WHERE TO APPLY. Application information as well as a copy of the "Journalism Scholarship Guide" (available at no charge) may be obtained by writing to:

The Newspaper Fund
P. O. Box 300
Princeton, New Jersey 08540

INTERN SCHOLARSHIP PROGRAM

ELIGIBILITY. Students who are college juniors working on school newspapers are eligible for scholarships and summer employment in the Reporting Intern Program or the Editing Intern Program.

AMOUNT OF ASSISTANCE. Scholarships of $500 and summer employment (between the junior and senior years in college) are available for students entering the Reporting Intern Program. Students entering the Editing Intern Program may receive scholarships of $700, summer employment (between the junior and senior years in college), and a three-week intensive journalism course.

WHERE TO APPLY. Application deadline is mid-November. Information and application forms may be obtained by writing to:

The Newspaper Fund
P. O. Box 300
Princeton, New Jersey 08540

14. COOPER UNION FULL-TUITION SCHOLARSHIP PROGRAM

PROVIDES full-tuition scholarships to The Cooper Union, a college in New York.

ELIGIBILITY. Student must be a resident of the United States and a graduate of an approved secondary school. Scholarship awards are competitive.

AMOUNT OF ASSISTANCE. Assistance is in the form of tuition-free day and evening professional courses leading to degrees in architecture, art, engineering, and science, or to certificates in art at The Cooper Union, which is a privately endowed and independent college in New York.

WHERE TO APPLY. Application information may be obtained by writing to:

The Cooper Union for the Advancement
  of Science and Art
Cooper Square
New York, New York 10003

15. WILLIAM RANDOLPH HEARST FOUNDATION JOURNALISM SCHOLARSHIP AWARDS PROGRAM

PROVIDES scholarships to undergraduate students majoring in journalism.

ELIGIBILITY. Any student majoring in journalism who is a candidate for a degree at a college or university that is a member of the American Association of Schools and Departments of Journalism is eligible. Scholarships will be awarded to students in recognition of outstanding performance in college and university journalism.

AMOUNT OF ASSISTANCE. Scholarship amounts vary.

WHERE TO APPLY. Application information may be obtained by writing to:

The William Randolph Hearst Foundation
Suite 218, Hearst Building
Third and Market Streets
San Francisco, California 94103

16. COAL COMPANY SCHOLARSHIP PROGRAM

PROVIDES scholarships for college education.

ELIGIBILITY. Some of the scholarships have no restrictions, while other scholarships have specific eligibility requirements, such as majoring in a certain subject, attending a certain school, being the son or daughter of a company employee, or living in a certain state or area.

AMOUNT OF ASSISTANCE. Varies from $100 to $1,500 per academic year.

WHERE TO APPLY. Application information may be obtained by writing to:

National Coal Association
1130 Seventeenth Street, N.W.
Washington, D.C. 20036

17. NATIONAL 4-H SCHOLARSHIP AWARDS PROGRAM

PROVIDES scholarships to encourage boys and girls to continue their education beyond high school.

ELIGIBILITY. Students must be 4-H members to be eligible for most scholarships, although some scholarships are available to former 4-H members. In addition, participants must meet the requirements established by the respective state extension services. There are other specific eligibility requirements for some of the awards. Further information may be obtained by writing to the State 4-H Leader.

AMOUNT OF ASSISTANCE. Scholarship amounts vary.

WHERE TO APPLY. Scholarship information may be obtained from the local 4-H Leader, or the State 4-H Leader, or by writing to:

National 4-H Service Committee, Inc.
59 East Van Buren Street
Chicago, Illinois 60605

18. DENTAL STUDENTS FINANCIAL AID PROGRAM

PROVIDES financial assistance to students pursuing an education in dentistry or in one of its related fields.

ELIGIBILITY. Students in need of financial assistance to pursue an education in dentistry or in one of its related fields are eligible. Generally, student loans are made on the basis of academic achievement and need.

AMOUNT OF ASSISTANCE. Amounts of scholarships and loans vary.

WHERE TO APPLY. Application information may be obtained by writing to one of these sources:

ARIZONA
Arizona State Dental Association
Student Loan Fund
3800 N. Central Avenue
Phoenix, Arizona 85012

DELAWARE
Delaware Academy of Medicine, Inc.
Scholarship Loan Fund
1925 Lovering Avenue
Wilmington, Delaware 19806

FLORIDA
Florida State Dental Society
Student Loan Fund
P. O. Box 18105
Tampa, Florida 33609

INDIANA
Indiana State Dental Association
Student Loan Fund Program
721 Hume Mansur Building
Indianapolis, Indiana 46204

IOWA
IDA Student Loan Fund
University of Iowa Foundation
Iowa Memorial Union
Iowa City, Iowa 52240

University of Iowa Achievement Fund
Iowa Memorial Union
Iowa City, Iowa 52240

KANSAS
Kansas State Dental Auxiliary Loan
Fund
School of Dentistry
University of Missouri at Kansas City
Kansas City, Missouri 64110

KENTUCKY
Kentucky State Board of Dental
Examiners
Rural Scholarship (Kentucky Dental)
2106 Bardstown Road
Louisville, Kentucky 40205

Memorial Student Loan Fund
Kentucky Dental Association
1940 Princeton Drive
Louisville, Kentucky 40205

LOUISIANA
Women's Auxiliary to the Louisiana
Dental Association
Dental Student Loan Fund
10 Stilt Street
New Orleans, Louisiana 70124

MAINE
Maine Dental Association Student
Loan Fund
Bethel, Maine 04217

MASSACHUSETTS
Massachusetts Dental Society
Dental Student Financial Aid Committee
The Prudential Tower Building
Suite 4318
Boston, Massachusetts 02199

South Shore District Dental Society
Loan Fund
47 West Elm Street
Brockton, Massachusetts 02401

MINNESOTA
Minnesota State Dental Association
Student Loan Fund
2236 Marshall Avenue
St. Paul, Minnesota 55104

NEBRASKA
The Dr. Clyde W. Davis Student Loan
Fund
University of Nebraska
Office of Scholarships and Financial
Aids
Administration Building 205
Lincoln, Nebraska 68508

NEVADA
Nevada State Dental Society
Loan Fund
P. O. Box 646
Sparks, Nevada 89431

NEW HAMPSHIRE
MacRury Scholarship Fund for Dental
   Hygiene Students*
188 Cody Street
Manchester, New Hampshire 03103
Walter F. Winchester and New Hamp-
   shire Dental Society
Memorials Scholarship Fund
Chairman, Scholarship Fund Commit-
   tee
19 Temple Court
Manchester, New Hampshire 03104

NEW JERSEY
Scholarship and Loan Committee
Bergen County Dental Society
Englewood, New Jersey 07631

NEW MEXICO
New Mexico Dental Association†
Student Loan Fund
2917 Santa Cruz Avenue, S.E.
Albuquerque, New Mexico 87106

NORTH CAROLINA
Charlotte Dental Auxiliary‡
Dental Student Loan Fund
North Carolina Dental Society
P. O. Box 11065
Raleigh, North Carolina 27604

Fifth District Dental Auxiliary§
Dental Assistant Student Loan Pro-
   gram
North Carolina Dental Society
P. O. Box 11065
Raleigh, North Carolina 27604

North Carolina Dental Society
Dental Student Loan Fund
P. O. Box 11065
Raleigh, North Carolina 27604

OKLAHOMA
Oklahoma Dental Foundation for Re-
   search and Education
222 Plaza Court Building
Oklahoma City, Oklahoma 73112

SOUTH CAROLINA
South Carolina Dental Association Student Loan
1506 Gregg Street
Columbia, South Carolina 29201

TENNESSEE
L. G. Noel Memorial Foundation
Student Loan Fund
307 East F Street
Elizabethton, Tennessee 37643

VERMONT
Dr. C. I. Taggart Memorial Fund*
University of Vermont
590 Main Street
Burlington, Vermont 05401

VIRGINIA
Dental Hygienists' Scholarship-Loan
   Funds*
Virginia State Dental Association
18 North Fifth Street
Richmond, Virginia 23219

Virginia State Dental Association
Student Loan Fund
Medical College of Virginia
School of Dentistry
521 North Eleventh Street
Richmond, Virginia 23219

WASHINGTON
Women's Auxiliary†
Washington State Dental Association
   Scholarship Fund
417 Grosvenor House
500 Wall Street
Seattle, Washington 98121

WEST VIRGINIA
Auxiliary of the West Virginia State
   Dental Society
Dental School Loan Fund
School of Dentistry
West Virginia University
The Medical Center
Morgantown, West Virginia 26506

* Dental hygiene students only
* Dental or dental hygiene students only
‡ Dental, dental hygiene or dental assisting stu-
dents only
§ Dental assisting students only

WISCONSIN
Wisconsin Dental Association Foundation
Student Loan Fund
633 W. Wisconsin Avenue
Milwaukee, Wisconsin 53203

Additionally, limited scholarships and loans are available through the following organizations:

American Dental Assistants' Association
211 East Chicago Avenue
Chicago, Illinois 60611

American Dental Hygienists' Association
211 East Chicago Avenue
Chicago, Illinois 60611

(For dental laboratory technology scholarships)
American Fund for Dental Education
211 East Chicago Avenue
Chicago, Illinois 60611

Information regarding the following loans can be obtained from the School of Dentistry, University of Minnesota, Washington Avenue and Union Street, S.E., Minneapolis, Minnesota 55455:

Duluth District Auxiliary Loan Fund
Minneapolis District Auxiliary Loan Fund
Northwestern District Auxiliary Loan Fund
St. Paul District Auxiliary Loan Fund
Southeastern District Loan Fund

19. DENTAL SCHOLARSHIPS FOR UNDERGRADUATE DISADVANTAGED MINORITY STUDENTS

PROVIDES scholarship grants to qualified students pursuing studies in dental education.

ELIGIBILITY. Student must be a United States citizen from a minority group that is currently underrepresented in the dental profession. This would include, in particular, blacks, Mexican Americans, American Indians, and Puerto Ricans. In addition, the student must be entering his final year of predental studies.

AMOUNT OF ASSISTANCE. Scholarship grants are annual, are for amounts of up to $2,500 per year (depending on need), and are renewable provided the student has met all of the requirements for continuation of his studies. A total of up to $12,500 may be granted over a five-year period. This includes the final year of predental study and four years of dental school.

WHERE TO APPLY. Application information may be obtained by writing to:

American Fund for Dental Education
Suite 1630
211 East Chicago Avenue
Chicago, Illinois 60611

20. LIBRARY EDUCATION FINANCIAL ASSISTANCE PROGRAM

PROVIDES financial assistance to students pursuing studies in library education.

ELIGIBILITY. The student must meet the eligibility requirements of the source of assistance. Such requirements vary from being accepted for enrollment in the undergraduate program to specifying intention to qualify as a school librarian or to work in a public library of a particular state, etc.

AMOUNT OF ASSISTANCE. There are numerous scholarships, grants, and loans available in varying amounts.

WHERE TO APPLY. Application information may be obtained from guidance counselors and librarians, or from the financial aid officer of the college or university you attend or plan to attend. A booklet entitled *Financial Assistance for Library Education* which includes sources, types and amounts of assistance, and where to apply may be obtained by writing to the following address and including a self-addressed mailing label:

Library Education Division
American Library Association
50 East Huron Street
Chicago, Illinois 60611

21. INDEPENDENT UNIONS AND AFL-CIO AFFILIATED LABOR UNIONS SCHOLARSHIP AWARDS PROGRAMS

PROVIDES financial aid to children of members, and young union members to acquire an education beyond the high school level.

ELIGIBILITY. Children of members of labor unions and young union members are eligible. In addition, some scholarship awards are available also to any high school student, whether or not a son or daughter of a union member, so long as the student can meet special eligibility requirements that such awards may specify.

AMOUNT OF ASSISTANCE. Awards range from $100 to scholarships worth $10,000 for four college years. Scholarships are in one of two categories: (1) those of national and international unions awarded on a national basis, and (2) those of state councils, districts, and local unions.

WHERE TO APPLY. Application information is contained in a booklet entitled *Student Aid Bulletin* which has a listing of these union scholarships. This booklet is available (for a fee of $2.00) from the address listed below:

CHRONICLE GUIDANCE Publications, Inc.
Moravia, New York 13118

Part III

SELECTED STATE UNDERGRADUATE STUDENT ASSISTANCE PROGRAMS

ALABAMA

PROGRAM	AMOUNT OF ASSISTANCE
Alabama GI and Dependents Educational Benefit Act	Free instructional fees and tuition, from 18 to 36 months maximum; for certain widows and wives of living veterans, 18 months maximum (available in addition to federal government benefits)
Alabama War Chest Scholarships (children of veterans)	Scholarships up to $300 per year; $400 per year for medical and dental students at 8 state colleges and University of Alabama
Dental Scholarship Loans	(a) Scholarship loans, $2,000 per year (for up to 4 years)
	(b) Merit scholarships, $2,000 each
Medical Scholarship Loans	(a) Scholarship loans, $2,000 per year (for up to 4 years)
	(b) Merit scholarships, $2,000 each
Elementary Teacher Scholarships	Up to $100 per year

66

ELIGIBILITY	WHERE TO APPLY
Provides for widows and children of deceased veterans; and wives and children of veterans partially disabled during certain war periods; also dependents of prisoners of war and those missing in action	Department of Veterans Affairs P. O. Box 1509 Montgomery, Alabama 36102, or in any county Veterans' Service Office
Must be in upper 50 percent of high school or college class, need financial assistance, and have parent who entered Armed Forces from state of Alabama to serve in World War II with not less than 6 months' service prior to December 1945	Financial aids office of the college or university you plan to attend (refer to Alabama War Chest Scholarship)
(a) Any resident of Alabama of good character who has been accepted for matriculation at the University of Alabama in Birmingham School of Dentistry or a comparable institution (preference given to those who show need)	Board of Dental Scholarship Awards 1919 Seventh Avenue, So. Birmingham, Alabama 35233
(b) Application not made by student; granted solely on basis of scholastic qualification and awarded by Board of Dental Scholarship Awards, for students enrolled at the University of Alabama School of Dentistry	Board of Dental Scholarship Awards 1919 Seventh Avenue, So. Birmingham, Alabama 35233
(a) Any resident of Alabama of good character who has been accepted for matriculation at the Medical College of Alabama or a comparable institution (preference given to those who show need)	State of Alabama Board of Medical Scholarship Awards 1600 8th Avenue, So. University Station Birmingham, Alabama 35294
(b) Application not made by student; granted solely on basis of scholastic qualification and awarded by Board of Medical Scholarship Awards	State of Alabama Board of Medical Scholarship Awards 1600 8th Avenue, So. University Station Birmingham, Alabama 35294
Based on financial need and must plan to teach 3 years in Alabama elementary schools	Florence State University, Jacksonville State University, Livingston University, or Troy State University Student Aids Office

PROGRAM	AMOUNT OF ASSISTANCE
Scholarships for Children of Blind Parents	Fees and tuition at state-supported institutions (36 months maximum)
Social Work Grants	Up to $1,800 per year
Guaranteed Loans	Up to $1,500 per year
Tuskegee Nursing Scholarships	Varies; assistance is in the form of reduced tuition
Veterans (Vietnam era)	Free correspondence or extension courses from state-supported schools

ALASKA

Guaranteed Loans	Up to $2,500 per year
Law Enforcement Education Program	Loans of up to $1,800 per year; some grants
"Native" Alaskan Scholarships	Fees; room and board
State Room Scholarships	Dormitory rent for 2 years
State Scholarship Loans	Up to $2,500 for an undergraduate

ELIGIBILITY	WHERE TO APPLY
Children of blind head of household whose family income is less than $3,000	Division of Rehabilitation and Crippled Children State Board of Education Montgomery, Alabama 36104
Preference given to applicants from counties with a shortage of social workers	School of Social Work University of Alabama University, Alabama 35486
Approved by local lending institutions and colleges	Local lending institutions
Qualified applicants at Tuskegee Institute who are Alabama residents	Tuskegee Institute Tuskegee Institute, Alabama 36088
Certain Vietnam era veterans who qualify	State Department of Veteran Affairs P. O. Box 1509 Montgomery, Alabama 36102, or any county Veterans' Service officer of that department
Approval by college and lending institution	United Student Aid Funds, Inc. 5259 N. Tacoma Avenue Indianapolis, Indiana 46220
Residents of Alaska enrolled in program leading to degree in law enforcement, law probation and parole, or penology	Commissioner of Public Safety State Capitol, Pouch N Juneau, Alaska 99801
Students of one-quarter or more Alaskan "native" origin; preference given to residents of rural Alaska who entered to become teachers; based on need	Financial Aid Office Box 95167 University of Alaska Fairbanks, Alaska 99701
Highest-ranking senior in each Alaskan high school	Financial Aid Office Box 95167 University of Alaska Fairbanks, Alaska 99701
Resident of Alaska for 2 years, high school graduate or equivalent enrolled, or accepted for enrollment, full-time in approved or accredited school; based on financial need	Student Loan Office Alaska Department of Education Alaska Office Building, Pouch F Juneau, Alaska 99801

PROGRAM	AMOUNT OF ASSISTANCE
Talent Grants	$1,400 per year for Alaska residents; $1,700 for nonresidents

ARIZONA

Activity Scholarships	Varies
Guaranteed Loan Program	Up to $1,500 per year
Indian Scholarships	Varies
Regents Scholarship	Varies
Law Enforcement Education Loans and Grants	(a) Loans not to exceed $1,800 per year
	(b) Grants not to exceed $300 per semester
Nursing Student Loans and Scholarships	Up to $1,500 per year

ELIGIBILITY	WHERE TO APPLY
Students with outstanding potential in creative writing, certain sports, drama, music, and art	Financial Aid Office Box 95167 University of Alaska Fairbanks, Alaska 99701
Proficiency demonstrated in areas required by the institution such as music, athletics, etc.	Board of Regents Arizona State Office Phoenix, Arizona 85007 (or individual college student plans to attend)
Approval by college and lending institution	Local lending institution
American Indian students at Arizona State University who show scholastic attainment, character, promise of success in chosen field, and based on financial need	Scholarships and Financial Aid Committee Arizona State University Tempe, Arizona 85281
Based on financial need and scholastic achievement	Board of Regents Arizona State Office Phoenix, Arizona 85007 or Scholarships and Financial Aid Committee Arizona State University Tempe, Arizona 85281
(a) Loans restricted to full-time students enrolled, or accepted for enrollment, in degree program in area directly related to law enforcement	Scholarships and Financial Aid Committee Arizona State University Tempe, Arizona 85281
(b) Grants restricted to in-service law enforcement officers of local, state, or designated unit of the federal government; student may be full- or part-time	Scholarships and Financial Aid Committee Arizona State University Tempe, Arizona 85281
Enrolled as full-time student in course leading to baccalaureate degree in nursing; have good scholastic standing, and show financial need	Scholarships and Financial Aid Committee, Arizona State University Tempe, Arizona 85281

PROGRAM	AMOUNT OF ASSISTANCE
Special Scholarships	Varies

ARKANSAS

Academic, Athletic, Music, Speech, and Drama Scholarships	Varies
Guaranteed Loan Program	Up to $1,000 per year

CALIFORNIA

Dependents of Deceased or Disabled Veterans	$50 monthly plus tuition within certain limits
State Scholarships	Up to $2,000 per year
University of Southern California General University Scholarships	In most cases, the maximum value is a grant of full tuition credit for an academic year

ELIGIBILITY	WHERE TO APPLY
Some based on financial need, some awarded by sponsoring firm or individual donor, some left to discretion of Arizona State University Scholarships Committee; student may apply for Special and Regents Scholarships concurrently	Scholarships and Financial Aid Committee Arizona State University Tempe, Arizona 85281
Academic excellence and ability to excel in required activity area	Dean of Students, Drawer G, State University, Arkansas 72467 or State College of Arkansas Conway, Arkansas 72032
Endorsement by university in which the student is enrolled, or accepted for enrollment, and family adjusted income is less than $15,000 per year	Hometown lending agency
Wives, widows, and children of veterans whose death or disability was the result of service	Department of Veterans Affairs Division of Veteran Services 350 McAllister Street San Francisco, California 94102
Qualified students who demonstrate financial need, high moral character, and good citizenship	State Scholarship and Loan Commission 714 P Street, Suite 1640 Sacramento, California 95814
Entering freshmen, junior-college transfers, and current University of Southern California students; minimum "B" grade average required; must show financial need	Director, Office of Student Aid Student Union 201 University of Southern California Los Angeles, California 90007

COLORADO

PROGRAM	AMOUNT OF ASSISTANCE
Boettcher Foundation Scholarships	Tuition, books, and $1,000 per year
Dental Tuition Grants	Difference between resident and nonresident tuition plus small travel allowance
Federally Insured Student Loan Program	Up to $2,500 per year
Colorado Student Grants and Scholarships	Up to $1,000 based on documented need; no-need awards limited to $100
Career Education Grant	Up to $300 per year
Minority Teacher Incentive Scholarships	Up to $1,000 per year
Colorado Work-Study	Varies according to need

CONNECTICUT

Guaranteed Loans	Up to $1,500 per year

ELIGIBILITY	WHERE TO APPLY
Resident of Colorado for 2 years prior to graduation from high school; be in upper 10 percent of graduating class	Boettcher Foundation 800 Boston Building 828 Seventeenth Street Denver, Colorado 80202
Student must be enrolled, or accepted for enrollment, in an accredited dental school in the United States	Colorado Dental Committee University of Colorado Medical Center 4200 East Ninth Avenue Denver, Colorado 80220
U.S. citizen or national who is enrolled, or accepted for enrollment, on at least a half-time basis at an eligible school	Local lending institution, or eligible schools
Be enrolled, or accepted for enrollment, at a Colorado public institution; limited funds available for nonresident students.	Financial aid officer of the college you plan to attend
Must show aptitude for chosen career	Colorado Congress of Parents and Teachers 1441 Welton Street Denver, Colorado 80202
Colorado resident, upper division of graduating class; financial need; member of minority population	Financial aid officer at institution where student plans to attend.
Colorado resident, undergraduate, show financial need; 30 percent of funds appropriated are utilized to provide job opportunities for students on a basis other than need	Financial aid officer at institution you plan to attend
Approval by the lending institution and the college	Your local bank or lending institution

PROGRAM	AMOUNT OF ASSISTANCE
Nursing Awards	Varies
Orphans or Dependents of Disabled Veterans	Up to $200 per year
Restricted Educational Achievement Program	Up to $1,000 per year
State College Scholarships	Up to $300 per year
Connecticut State Scholarships	From $100 to $1,000 per year
Tuition Fees Fund	About $100 per year
University of Connecticut Trustee Scholarships	Varies

DELAWARE

Financial Aid Program of the University of Delaware	Varies
Guaranteed Loans	Up to $1,500 per year
Orphans of Veterans	Up to $500 per year

ELIGIBILITY	WHERE TO APPLY
Must be enrolled, or accepted for enrollment, in a Connecticut nursing education program, be a Connecticut resident for 4 years, and agree to apply for a Connecticut license and practice in the state following licensure	State Board of Examiners for Nursing 79 Elm Street Hartford, Connecticut 06115
Children of deceased or disabled veterans	Commission for Higher Education P. O. Box 1320 Hartford, Connecticut 06115
Certain educationally disadvantaged students of financial need	State Scholarship Commission and Commission for Higher Education P. O. Box 1320 Hartford, Connecticut 06115
Student must be preparing to teach; based on scholarship and financial need	Directly to the state college
Awarded on the basis of CEEB scores, scholastic record, and financial need; must be resident of Connecticut	State Scholarship Commission 340 Capital Avenue Hartford, Connecticut 06115
Student at a state college; based on exceptional promise and need	Directly to the state college
Worthy students in need of financial assistance	Directly to the University of Connecticut
Students enrolled, or accepted for enrollment, at University of Delaware who are best qualified in terms of need and merit	Office of Financial Aid 207 Hullihen Hall University of Delaware Newark, Delaware 19711
Approval by college and lending institution, and be a resident of Delaware	Your local bank or lending institution
Child (16 to 25 years of age) of deceased war veteran who was killed or died as a result of various wars.	State Director Vocational Education Division State Board of Education Department of Public Instruction Dover, Delaware 19901

PROGRAM	AMOUNT OF ASSISTANCE
Scholarship Fund	Up to $800 per year

DISTRICT OF COLUMBIA

War Orphans' Assistance Program	Up to $200 per year for tuition, fees, books, etc.

FLORIDA

Scholarships for Children of Deceased or Disabled Veterans	$375 per academic year
Confederate Memorial Scholarships	$150 per academic year
Florida Student Loans	Up to $1,200 per academic year
Optometry Scholarship Loans	Up to $1,000 per year
Student Assistance Grants	Up to $1,200 per academic year

ELIGIBILITY	WHERE TO APPLY
Delaware resident students pursuing degrees outside the state not available in Delaware state institutions; based on need, academic qualifications, and probability of employment in Delaware	Scholarship Advisory Council Care of State Board of Education Dover, Delaware 19901
Child, 16 to 21 years of age, of veteran parent who was killed or died as a result of service during certain war periods	Superintendent of Public Schools of District of Columbia Presidential Building 415 12th Street, N.W. Washington, D.C. 20004
Dependent children of deceased or disabled veterans and servicemen who are prisoners of war or missing in action; funds may be used only at state universities and public community colleges in Florida; 5-year Florida residency	Scholarships and Loans Section Department of Education Tallahassee, Florida 32304 or Division of Veterans Affairs P. O. Box 1437 St. Petersburg, Florida 33731
Certified lineal descendant of Confederate soldier or sailor; funds may be used only at state universities or public community colleges in Florida; Florida residency required	Scholarships and Loans Section Department of Education Tallahassee, Florida 32304
Based on financial need; Florida residency; must be for attendance at a college or university in Florida	Scholarships and Loans Section Department of Education Tallahassee, Florida 32304
Resident of Florida for not less than 5 years; be accepted for admission to a fully accredited optometric college	Florida State Board of Optometry 547 North Monroe Street Tallahassee, Florida 32304
Capable Florida students with exceptional financial need; 2 years' Florida residency; must attend accredited college or university in Florida	Scholarships and Loans Section Department of Education Tallahassee, Florida 32304

PROGRAM	AMOUNT OF ASSISTANCE
Seminole and Miccosukee Indian Scholarships	Up to $600 per academic year

GEORGIA

Guaranteed Student Loans	Up to $1,200 per year
Medical Scholarships	Up to $2,500 per year
State Scholarship Commission Awards	Varies
Regents Scholarships	Up to $750 per year

HAWAII

Student Loan Guarantee Program	Up to $1,500 per year
Health Professions Scholarships	Up to $2,500 per year
Nursing Scholarships	Up to $1,500 per year

Seminole or Miccosukee Indian residents of Florida; based on competitive examination and demonstrated financial need; must attend Florida institution	Scholarships and Loans Section Department of Education Tallahassee, Florida 32304, or Bureau of Indian Affairs Seminole Indian Agency Hollywood, Florida 33024
Applications certified by college; loan approved by lending institution and guaranteed by state of Georgia	Georgia Higher Education Assistance Corporation P. O. Box 38005 Atlanta, Georgia 30334
Acceptance at an accredited medical college and have financial need	State Medical Education Board 244 Washington Street, S.W. Atlanta, Georgia 30334
Enrollment in an approved professional, educational, or paramedical field and have financial need	State Scholarship Commission Room 703 270 Washington Street, S.W. Atlanta, Georgia 30334
Based on financial need and scholastic ability	Director of student aid at the institution in the university system of Georgia that the applicant plans to attend
Approval of college, state, and lending institution	Department of Budget and Finance State Office Building P. O. Box 150 Honolulu, Hawaii 96810
Enrolled as a full-time student in School of Medicine at University of Hawaii and have exceptional financial need	Financial Aids Office University of Hawaii 1627 A Bachman Place Honolulu, Hawaii 96822
Enrolled as a full-time student in School of Nursing at University of Hawaii and have exceptional financial need	Financial Aids Office University of Hawaii 1627 A Bachman Place Honolulu, Hawaii 96822

PROGRAM	AMOUNT OF ASSISTANCE
State Scholarship Program	Varies

IDAHO

Freshman Honorary Scholarships	$160 per year
Guaranteed Student Loans	Up to $1,500 per year
Music Scholarships	(a) Associated students of the University of Idaho Activities Scholarships: $300 (a few are renewable for 1 year) (b) String Quartet Scholarships: $300–$500 (renewable for 4 years) (c) Marching Band Work-Performance Scholarships: $100 (primarily to upper-classmen) (d) School of Music Scholarships: $50–$500 (occasionally renewable)

ILLINOIS

Agriculture and Home Economics Scholarships	Tuition waiver at University of Illinois
Children of Veterans Scholarships	Tuition at University of Illinois
County Scholarships	Tuition at Illinois state-supported colleges and universities
Illinois Department of Children and Family Services	Limited room and board stipends for wards of the Department; tuition scholarships must be obtained by the student

ELIGIBILITY	WHERE TO APPLY
Based on financial need and scholastic ability	Financial Aids Office University of Hawaii 1627 A Bachman Place Honolulu, Hawaii 96822
Students who have graduated from an Idaho high school and have academic ability and financial need	Scholarships, Awards, and Prizes Committee Idaho State University Pocatello, Idaho 83201
Approval by college, state, and local lending institution	Local lending institution
Financial need, contribution (realized or potential) to the department, and academic record	Director of Financial Aids, and the Director of the School of Music University of Idaho Moscow, Idaho 83843
Be resident of county in which application is made and based on ACT scores	Local county superintendent of schools
Child of veteran, reside in county where application is filed, and based on ACT scores	High school principal, or local county superintendent of schools
Reside in county where application is made, and based on ACT scores	Local county superintendent of schools
Ward of the Department who is academically qualified for higher education	Illinois Department of Children and Family Services, Springfield, Illinois 62706

PROGRAM	AMOUNT OF ASSISTANCE
General Assembly Scholarships	Varies
Special Education Grants	Varies
Monetary Award Program	Up to $1,200 per year
Illinois Guaranteed Loan Program	Up to $1,000 for freshman year; $1,500 for each academic level thereafter to a maximum of $7,500
Veterans' Scholarships	Tuition waiver

INDIANA

Child of Disabled Veteran Award	Remits a portion of the instructional fees
Federally Insured Loan Program	Up to $1,500 per year
La Verne Noyes Awards	$125 per year

ELIGIBILITY	WHERE TO APPLY
Be resident of district that is represented by a member of the General Assembly	Local member of the General Assembly
Must agree to work in field of special education one-half year for each year of grant	Department of Scholarship Services 212 E. Monroe Street Springfield, Illinois 62706
Be a resident of Illinois and show financial need	Illinois State Scholarship Commission P. O. Box 607 Deerfield, Illinois 60015
Be a resident of Illinois; approval by college, state, and local lending institution	Illinois Guaranteed Loan Program Box 33 Deerfield, Illinois 60015
Available to certain honorably discharged Armed Service veterans	University of Illinois (Urbana-Champaign) Student Financial Aid Office Room 109 707 South Sixth Street Champaign, Illinois 61820
Child of a veteran of World War I, World War II, Korean Conflict, or Vietnam era; father must have suffered a service-connected disability or death; student must have been resident of Indiana for the immediate previous year	State college you plan to attend
Approval by college, state, and local lending institution	College Student Loan Program Indiana State Scholarship Commission Room 514 State Office Building Indianapolis, Indiana 46204
Students must be blood descendants of service members of World War I who enlisted prior to May 11, 1918, or served overseas after that date, and must show financial need	Indiana University Office of Scholarships and Financial Aid 809 East Seventh Street Bloomington, Indiana, 47401

PROGRAM	AMOUNT OF ASSISTANCE
State Scholarships	Varies from $100 to $1,400 per year
Residence Scholarship Program	Varies
Indiana University Scholarships	Varies
Indiana University Grants Program	Varies
Indiana University Distinguished Scholarship Program	Varies

IOWA

Disabled Persons	Varies
Grants for Lower- and Middle-Income Students	Varies
Guaranteed Student Loans	Up to $1,500 per year

Based on financial need, high school rank, and SAT scores	State Scholarship Commission Room 514 State Office Building Indianapolis, Indiana 46204
High academic potential and exceptional need	Indiana University Office of Scholarships and Financial Aid 809 East Seventh Street Bloomington, Indiana 47401
High academic potential and exceptional need	Indiana University Office of Scholarships and Financial Aid 809 East Seventh Street Bloomington, Indiana 47401
Students who show exceptional financial need	Indiana University Office of Scholarships and Financial Aid 809 East Seventh Street Bloomington, Indiana 47401
Have shown superior academic performance; given some service to community, school, and/or church, and be recommended by principal, teacher, etc.	Indiana University Office of Scholarships and Financial Aid 809 East Seventh Street, Bloomington, Indiana 47401
Must have physical or mental disability that is a handicap to employment	Rehabilitation Education and Service 801 Bankers Trust Building Des Moines, Iowa 50309
Based on financial need	Iowa Higher Education Facilities Commission 201 Jewett Building Des Moines, Iowa 50309
Approval by college, state, and local lending institution	Iowa Higher Education Facilities Commission 201 Jewett Building Des Moines, Iowa 50309

PROGRAM	AMOUNT OF ASSISTANCE
Iowa State University General Scholarships	Varies
Iowa Medical Tuition Loans	$870 to $2,000 for tuition at Iowa medical and osteopathic colleges; may be canceled for service in the state
State of Iowa Scholarships	$100 to $610 per year
University of Iowa Merit Freshmen Tuition Scholarships	$100 to full resident tuition
University of Northern Iowa Student Aid	Varies up to $528 per year
War Orphans' Assistance	Up to $400 per year

KANSAS

State Scholarships	Up to $500 per year

Based on financial need and academic ability	Iowa State University of Science and Technology Office of Student Financial Aids Beardshear Hall Ames, Iowa 50010
Any Iowa resident studying to be a doctor who plans to practice general medicine in Iowa for at least 5 years after training	Iowa Higher Education Facilities Commission 201 Jewett Building Des Moines, Iowa 50309
Based on financial need and academic ability	Iowa Higher Education Facilities Commission 201 Jewett Building Des Moines, Iowa 50309
Rank in upper 10 percent of high school class; have composite ACT score of 28 or above, and have financial need	Office of Student Financial Aids 106 Old Dental Building University of Iowa Iowa City, Iowa 52240
Based on financial need, academic achievement, and an interest in teaching; must be a resident of Iowa	University of Northern Iowa Financial Aid Office Cedar Falls, Iowa 50613
Child of veteran who was killed or died as result of military service during certain war periods, or is prisoner of war or missing in action (Vietnam) on or after August 5, 1964	Iowa Bonus Board State House Des Moines, Iowa 50309
Based on class rank, scholastic achievement, and be a resident of Kansas	Kansas State Department of Education 120 East 10th Street Topeka, Kansas 66612

KENTUCKY

PROGRAM	AMOUNT OF ASSISTANCE
Children of Veterans	Varies
Dental Loan/Scholarships	Up to $1,500 per year
Medical Loan/Scholarships	Up to $2,500 per year
Disabled Student Assistance	Varies
Guaranteed Loan Program	Up to $1,500 per year
Honor Scholarships	Varies

LOUISIANA

Academic and Centennial Honor Scholarships	$200 to $800 per year
Alumni or Founders Scholarships	Varies
Athletic Scholarships	Varies
Baccalaureate Program for Nurses	Varies

ELIGIBILITY	WHERE TO APPLY
Children of veterans who died or are disabled as a result of military service during various wars	Student aid office at the college the applicant plans to attend
Acceptance at an accredited school of dentistry; must be a resident of Kentucky	Kentucky Dental Association 1940 Princeton Drive Louisville, Kentucky 40205
Acceptance at an accredited medical school; must be a resident of Kentucky	Rural Kentucky Medical Scholarship Fund Kentucky Medical Association 3532 Ephraim McDowell Drive Louisville, Kentucky 40205
Awards based on financial need, character, academic ability, and the presence of a disability that is a vocational handicap	Bureau of Rehabilitation State Department of Education State Office Building Frankfort, Kentucky 40601
Approval of college and the lending institution	Banks, credit unions, and savings and loan associations participating in the program
Based on financial need, academic ability, character, and citizenship	Student aid office at the state college the applicant plans to attend
Basis of academic and other achievement, class rank, testing, interviews, and recommendation of the high school principal	State Superintendent of Education Baton Rouge, Louisiana 70804
Competitive basis and other qualifying requirements vary	Student aid office at the public college or university the applicant plans to attend
Rank in upper one fourth to one third of graduating class and be recommended by high school principal	Student aid office at the college or university the applicant plans to attend.
Financial need and academic ability	Baccalaureate schools of nursing within the state

PROGRAM	AMOUNT OF ASSISTANCE
Children of Veterans	Varies
Departmental Scholarships	$20 per semester
Disabled Students	Varies
State Guaranteed Student Loan Program	Up to $1,000 per year
High School Honor Awards	Varies
High School Rally	One fourth to one third of the registration fee
Jaycees Merit Scholarships for Teaching	$250 to $2,000 per year
Music and Band Scholarships	Varies
Parish Loans	Up to $500 per year
Stonewall Jackson Scholarships	Up to $300 per year
T. H. Harris Scholarships	Up to $300 per year

Children of veterans who were killed, or died as a result of military service in World War I, World War II, Korean Conflict, or Vietnam era	Department of Veterans Affairs Louisiana National Bank Building Baton Rouge, Louisiana 70802
Worthy students who maintain good records	Available at most public colleges and universities
Financial need and academic ability	State Administrator Vocational Rehabilitation P. O. Box 44371 Baton Rouge, Louisiana 70804
Approval by college, state, and lending institution	Louisiana Higher Education 　Assistance Commission 2-B-3 Pentagon Courts Baton Rouge, Louisiana 70804
Be in upper one fourth to three fourths of graduating class and be recommended by the high school principal	High school principal
First-place winners in various contests in high school	High school principal
Awarded on competitive basis and must show financial need	Local Jaycees Club, or Louisiana Jaycees P. O. Box 637 Oaksdale, Louisiana 71463
Based on ability and promise as a performer	High school principal or band director, or music department of the college the applicant plans to attend
Requirements vary	Local parish, or superintendent of schools in your parish
Basis of an essay competition on Stonewall Jackson and scholastic achievement	Executive Secretary, Scholarship 　Program State Department of Education P. O. Box 44064 Baton Rouge, Louisiana 70804
Scholastic achievement and participation in extracurricular activities	Executive Secretary, Scholarship 　Program State Department of Education P. O. Box 44064 Baton Rouge, Louisiana 70804

93

MAINE

PROGRAM	AMOUNT OF ASSISTANCE
Guaranteed Loan Program	Up to $1,500 per year in accordance with federal statute
Teacher Scholarships	Up to $300 per year
University of Maine Scholarships	Varies
Vocational Technical Institute Scholarships	Up to $300 per year
War Orphans' Assistance	Up to $300 per year; free tuition at a Maine state-supported school at college or university level

MARYLAND

General State Scholarships	Up to $1,500 per year
Guaranteed Loan Program	Up to $1,250 per year
House of Delegates Scholarships	Waiver of tuition at University of Maryland, any Maryland state college, or public community college

ELIGIBILITY	WHERE TO APPLY
Approval by college, lending institution, and endorsement by United Student Aid Funds	Maine State Departmen of Education Augusta, Maine 04330
Enrollment in state college in Maine; have promise as a teacher; and have financial need	President of college, or student aid office in state college the applicant plans to attend
Financial need	Office of Student Financial Aid University of Maine, Orono Campus Orono, Maine 04473, or any of the six other University of Maine campuses
Awarded on basis of financial need and academic record	Director, S.M.V.T.I. South Portland, Maine 04106
Child, 16 to 21 years of age, whose parent was killed, or died, or is totally disabled as a result of service in various wars	Director of Guidance Division of Federal Resources State Department of Education Augusta, Maine 04330
Based upon financial need and SAT or ACT results; must be a Maryland resident	Local high school or college, or Maryland State Scholarship Board 2100 Guilford Avenue Baltimore, Maryland 21218
Approval by college, state, and lending institution	Maryland Higher Education Loan Corporation 2100 Guilford Avenue Baltimore, Maryland 21218
Appointment by member of the House of Delegates from your district	Maryland State Scholarship Board 2100 Guilford Avenue Baltimore, Maryland 21218, or member of House of Delegates from your district

95

PROGRAM	AMOUNT OF ASSISTANCE
Medical Scholarships	Up to $1,500 per year
Senatorial Scholarships	Up to $1,500 per year
State College Tuition Waiver	Waiver of tuition
Teacher Education Grants	Equivalent to tuition or fixed charges
War Orphans' Grants	Up to $500 per year
Professional School Scholarships	$200 to $1,000 for medicine, dentistry, law, nursing, and pharmacy
Children of Deceased Volunteer Firemen	Up to $500 per year

Eligibility	Where to Apply
Be admitted to the School of Medicine of University of Maryland, have financial need, agree to practice general medicine for 3 years in an area of need in the state, and have been a resident of Maryland for at least 5 years preceding date of award	Maryland State Scholarship Board 2100 Guilford Avenue Baltimore, Maryland 21218, or Dr. Karl Weaver University of Maryland School of Medicine College Park, Maryland 20740
Appointment by state senator on basis of SAT or ACT scores, and have financial need	Local high school or college, or Maryland State Scholarship Board 2100 Guilford Avenue Baltimore, Maryland 21218
Maryland residents, enrolled in the teacher preparation curriculum at Bowie, Coppin, Salisbury, or Towson State College	To the registrar of one of the four colleges mentioned
Maryland residents in the teacher education curriculum at Maryland and Morgan State Colleges and University of Maryland who agree to teach in Maryland schools for at least 2 years after graduation	To the registrar of one of the three institutions mentioned.
Child, 16 to 23 years of age, whose parent was a legal resident of Maryland prior to entering the Armed Forces and who was killed in action, or died, or was totally disabled as a result of service after December 7, 1941	Maryland State Scholarship Board 2100 Guilford Avenue Baltimore, Maryland 21218
Maryland student who has been a resident of the state for 3 years preceding date of award, and has been accepted for enrollment as a full-time student	Maryland State Scholarship Board 2100 Guilford Avenue Baltimore, Maryland 21218
Any child, 16 to 23 years of age, whose parent was a volunteer fireman in the state of Maryland and was killed in the line of duty	Firemen Association Rt. 1, Box 532 Frostburg, Maryland 21532

MASSACHUSETTS

PROGRAM	AMOUNT OF ASSISTANCE
Commonwealth Scholarships	Up to $250 per year
General State Scholarships	Up to $700 per year, and are renewable
Massachusetts Honor Scholarships	Tuition expenses at any 4-year institution supported by the Commonwealth of Massachusetts
Higher Education Loan Plan (HELP)	Up to $1,000 per year
Medical, Dental, and Nursing Scholarships	$200 to $700
Scholarships for Children of Deceased Members of Fire and Police Departments	Tuition waivers at state colleges for 4 years
Special Education Scholarships	Varies
University of Massachusetts Scholarships	Varies

ELIGIBILITY	WHERE TO APPLY
Awards based on competitive examination	Director of Financial Aid Lowell Technological Institute Lowell, Massachusetts 01854
Based on financial need	Board of Higher Education Scholarship Office 182 Tremont Street Boston, Massachusetts 02111
Solely on academic ability	High school or college counselor, or Board of Higher Education Scholarship Office 182 Tremont Street Boston, Massachusetts 02111

Approval by college, state, and lending institution	Massachusetts Higher Education
	   Assistance Corporation,
	511 Statler Building
	Boston, Massachusetts 02116, or
	   local lending institution

Awards based primarily on financial ability, but academic achievement also considered; must have permanent residence in Massachusetts	Board of Higher Education Scholarship Office 182 Tremont Street Boston, Massachusetts 02111
Parent who died as a result of injuries received in the performance of duty.	Board of Higher Education Scholarship Office 182 Tremont Street Boston, Massachusetts 02111
Must plan to teach mentally retarded; have financial need	Director of financial aid at college you plan to attend, or Board of Higher Education Scholarship Office 182 Tremont Street Boston, Massachusetts 02111
Needy and deserving students who have good scholastic records	Placement and Financial Aid Service Room 239, Whitmore Administration Building University of Massachusetts Amherst, Massachusetts 01002

PROGRAM	AMOUNT OF ASSISTANCE
Vietnam Veterans Assistance	Tuition waiver at state education institutions
War Orphans' Assistance	Up to $750 per year

MICHIGAN

Competitive Scholarships	Up to $800 per year
Guaranteed Loan	Up to $1,500 per year
Tuition Grants	Up to $800 per year
War Orphans' Education Assistance	Tuition, matriculation, and athletic fees at Michigan state-tax-supported colleges and universities

MINNESOTA

Bureau of Indian Affairs Scholarships	Varies; for 4 years

ELIGIBILITY	WHERE TO APPLY
Veterans who served in Vietnam for at least 80 days of active duty	Board of Higher Education Scholarship Office 182 Tremont Street Boston, Massachusetts 02111
Child, 16 to 24 years of age, of veteran parent who was killed or died as a result of service in various wars	Board of Higher Education Scholarship Office 182 Tremont Street Boston, Massachusetts 02111
Based on test scores and financial need	Bureau of Higher Education Michigan Department of Education P. O. Box 420 Lansing, Michigan 48902
Approval by college, lending institution, and state	Local lending institution, or Michigan Department of Education Division of Student Financial Aids P. O. Box 420 Lansing, Michigan 48902
Based on financial need and enrollment in approved private colleges in Michigan	Michigan Department of Education Division of Student Financial Aids P. O. Box 420 Lansing, Michigan 48902
Child, 16 to 22 years of age, of parent who was killed or died in any war, or is totally disabled (or has since died) from wartime service-incurred causes	Michigan Veterans Trust Fund Board of Trustees 122 S. Grand Avenue Lansing, Michigan 48913
One-quarter or more degree Indian ancestry, have financial need, and be recommended by the Minnesota Indian Scholarship Committee	Bureau of Indian Affairs Minneapolis Area Office 831 Second Avenue South Minneapolis, Minnesota 55402

101

PROGRAM	AMOUNT OF ASSISTANCE
Educational Assistance for Veterans	$250 for tuition
Nursing Grants-in-Aid	$2,000 maximum for R.N. program; $300 maximum for L.P.N. program
War Orphans' Educational Assistance	Up to $250 per year
State Grants-in-Aid	Up to $1,000 per year; renewable for 4 years of undergraduate study
State Scholarships	Up to $800 per year

MISSISSIPPI

Federally Insured Student Loan	Varies
State Medical Education Loan Program	Up to $1,250 per year
Out-of-State Scholarship Assistance	Varies

ELIGIBILITY	WHERE TO APPLY
Veterans who have exhausted federal GI Bill benefits	Veterans Benefit Division Department of Veterans Affairs Veterans Service Building St. Paul, Minnesota 55155
Based on financial need and ability	State Board of Nursing 393 North Dunlap Street St. Paul, Minnesota 55104
Lost veteran parent through death because of a service-caused condition	Veterans Benefit Division Department of Veterans Affairs Veterans Service Building St. Paul, Minnesota 55155
Admission to eligible institution and financial need	Minnesota Higher Education Coordinating Commission Suite 400, Capitol Square 550 Cedar Street St. Paul, Minnesota 55101
Based on scholastic achievement and financial need	Minnesota Higher Education Coordinating Commission Suite 400, Capitol Square 550 Cedar Street St. Paul, Minnesota 55101
Approval by college, lending institution, and U. S. Office of Education.	Board of Trustees of Institutions of Higher Learning 1855 Eastover Drive P. O. Box 2336 Jackson, Mississippi 39211
Enrolled, or accepted for enrollment, in approved medical school; must agree to practice for 5 years in a Board-approved community.	State Medical Education Loan Program P. O. Box 2336 Jackson, Mississippi 39205
Students who find it necessary to attend a professional or graduate institution to secure a degree in a field of study not available in Mississippi; must be resident of Mississippi	Board of Trustees of Institutions of Higher Learning 1855 Eastover Drive P. O. Box 2336 Jackson, Mississippi 39211

PROGRAM	AMOUNT OF ASSISTANCE
Regional Scholarships	Payment of out-of-state tuition for out-of-state students at Mississippi State University
Southern Regional Education Program	Varies

MISSOURI

Curators Scholars Program	Full waiver of incidental fees
Federally Insured Student Loan	Up to $1,500 per year
Merit and Regents Scholarships	Varies

MONTANA

Guaranteed Loans	Up to $1,500 per year
High School Honor Scholarships	Varies; approximately $270 per year, or $90 per quarter (for freshman year only)

ELIGIBILITY	WHERE TO APPLY
Based on standardized test scores and rank in high school graduation class.	Mississippi State University Office of Student Aid Drawer AB State College, Mississippi 39762
Enrollment at certain institutions in other states to study dentistry and veterinary medicine; must be resident of Mississippi	Board of Trustees of Institutions of Higher Learning 1855 Eastover Drive P. O. Box 2336 Jackson, Mississippi 39211
Selection of Missouri high school seniors based upon class rank and scores on a standardized test; must be recommended by high school counselor and/or principal	Director of Financial Aid Service Room 306, Clark Hall Columbia, Missouri 65201
Approval by college, lending institution, and U. S. Office of Education	Director of Higher Education Region VII 601 East 12th Street Kansas City, Missouri 64106
Awards based on class rank, financial need, and test scores	Director of student aid at the State College you plan to attend
Approval by college, lending institution, and U. S. Office of Education	Director of Higher Education Office of Education, Region VIII 9017 Federal Office Building 19th and Stout Streets Denver, Colorado 80202, or local lending institution
Awarded to high school graduating seniors who rank in the upper quarter of their class.	Your high school principal, or Executive Secretary, The Montana University System 1231 11th Avenue Helena, Montana 59601

PROGRAM	AMOUNT OF ASSISTANCE
Montana Fee Waiver Program for Indian Students	$90 per quarter in fee waivers with no limit on the number of quarters
Tuition Waiver for Nonresidents	Varies
Veterans' Scholarships	Registration, incidental, and departmental fees waived
War Orphans' Scholarships	Waiver of registration and incidental fees ($90 per quarter or $270 per year) so long as student is in school

NEBRASKA

Federally Insured Loans	Up to $2,500 per year
Regents Scholarships	Pays cost of 12 to 16 hours of resident tuition
Part-time Employment Program	$600 to $800
Rural Rehabilitation Endowment Fund Grant	Varies from $200 to $800 per year
War Orphans' Assistance	Waiver of tuition at a state college

ELIGIBILITY	WHERE TO APPLY
Students who have at least one-quarter degree Indian blood, have financial need, and are residents of Montana	Your high school Principal, or the financial aid officer at the unit of the Montana university system you plan to attend
Based on financial need, demonstrated scholarship, character, and promise	Financial aid office of the individual state college you plan to attend
Veterans who have exhausted their benefits and are no longer eligible under federal law	Financial aid office at the institution you plan to attend
Montana war orphan	Executive Secretary, The Montana University System 1231 11th Avenue Helena, Montana 59601
Accepted for admission and registered for classes	Office of Scholarships and Financial Aid 112 Administration Building University of Nebraska, Lincoln Lincoln, Nebraska 68508
Awarded on basis of competitive examination; must be a graduate of a Nebraska high school	High School principal/counselor, or Office of Scholarships and Financial Aid 112 Administration Building University of Nebraska, Lincoln Lincoln, Nebraska 68508
Be accepted for admission	Office of Scholarships and Financial Aid 112 Administration Building University of Nebraska, Lincoln Lincoln, Nebraska 68508
Farm or ranch youth who plans to attend state educational institution; based on financial need and scholastic achievement	Local Farmers Home Administration office, or Nebraska Department of Agriculture P. O. Box 4844, State Capitol Lincoln, Nebraska 68509
Child of veteran parent who died or was totally disabled as a result of service in the Armed Forces of the United States	Department of Veterans Affairs State Capitol Lincoln, Nebraska 68509

NEVADA

PROGRAM	AMOUNT OF ASSISTANCE
Fleishmann Scholarships	$1,000 for the freshman year of college study
Guaranteed Student Loans	Up to $1,500 per year
Registration Fee Waiver	Waiver of basic registration fee for that semester
Scholarships at State Universities	Varies
Tuition Waiver for Nonresidents	Waiver of nonresident tuition charge

NEW HAMPSHIRE

Guaranteed Student Loans	Up to $1,000 per year

ELIGIBILITY	WHERE TO APPLY
Programs are formulated and financed on a year-to-year basis and distributed to high school principals statewide	Your high school principal, or Scholarships Committee Max C. Fleishmann Foundation State Department of Education Carson City, Nevada 89701
Approval by college, lending institution, and U. S. Office of Education	Deputy Superintendent and Coordinator of Divisions Nevada State Department of Education Carson City, Nevada 89701
Based on scholastic achievement, financial need, and the rendering of special services to the university	Chairman, Scholarships and Prizes Board University of Nevada Reno, Nevada 89507, or Nevada Southern University Las Vegas, Nevada 89109
Awarded on basis of scholastic proficiency, need, character, service, and certain specialized talents	Chairman, Scholarships and Prizes Board University of Nevada Reno, Nevada 89507, or Nevada Southern University Las Vegas, Nevada 89109
Awarded to out-of-state residents on the basis of scholarship and service to the university	Chairman, Scholarships and Prizes Board University of Nevada Reno, Nevada 89507, or Nevada Southern University Las Vegas, Nevada 89109
Be a New Hampshire resident enrolled, or accepted for enrollment, at least half-time in an eligible institution	New Hampshire Higher Education Assistance Foundation 3 Capitol Street Concord, New Hampshire 03301, or local lending institution

109

PROGRAM	AMOUNT OF ASSISTANCE
Plymouth State College Merit Scholarships	$1,000
State Tuition Scholarships	Cover one half to full tuition costs
Scholarships for Orphans of Veterans	Waiver of tuition at any of the state post-secondary schools and up to $250 per year to defray costs

NEW JERSEY

Educational Opportunity Fund Grants	$250 to $1,000 per year; renewable annually for up to 6-year period
Guaranteed Student Loans	Up to $1,000 per year for freshman and sophomore years; $1,250 for junior year; $1,500 for senior year
Rehabilitation Commission Training Services	Varies; in addition to financial assistance, may include physical restoration, artificial appliances, psychotherapy, counseling, and placement
Educational Incentive Grants	$100 to $500 per year based upon tuition and fee charge
New Jersey State Scholarships	$500, or the cost of tuition, whichever is less

ELIGIBILITY	WHERE TO APPLY
High school graduates of exceptional ability and promise	Financial Aids Office Plymouth State College Plymouth, New Hampshire 03264
Based on financial need	Financial Aids Office Plymouth State College Plymouth, New Hampshire 03264
Child (legal resident of the state) 16 to 25 years of age, of veteran parent who died, or was killed as a result of service in various wars; such parent must have been a legal resident of the state at time of death	The state postsecondary school you plan to attend, or Department of Education 105 Loudon Road Concord, New Hampshire 03301
Economically and educationally disadvantaged students whose eligibility is determined by the college the student is attending or plans to attend; must have been resident of New Jersey at least 12 months prior to receiving grant	Your college financial aid office, or Educational Opportunity Fund Department of Higher Education 225 West State Street Trenton, New Jersey 08625
Approval by college, lending institution, and state; must be full-time student and resident of New Jersey	Local lending institution
Students who have a disability that substantially interferes with obtaining or retaining employment	New Jersey Rehabilitation Commission Department of Labor and Industry Labor and Industry Building John Fitch Plaza Trenton, New Jersey 08625
Any student who has received a state scholarship and plans to attend a college, university, or hospital school of nursing in New Jersey where tuition and fees exceed $500 per year	Department of Higher Education Office of Student Financial Aid 225 West State Street Trenton, New Jersey 08625
Competitively on basis of financial need and scholastic achievement; must have been a New Jersey resident for at least 12 months	High school counselor, or Department of Higher Education Office of Student Financial Aid 225 West State Street Trenton, New Jersey 08625

PROGRAM	AMOUNT OF ASSISTANCE
Tuition Aid Grants	$200 to $1,000 per year
War Orphans' Education Program	Up to $500 per year for 4 years

NEW MEXICO

Educational Opportunity Grants	$200 to $1,000 per year
Guaranteed Student Loans	Up to $2,500 per year
University of New Mexico Scholarships	Varies
War Orphans' Assistance	Waiver of tuition plus amount not to exceed $300 per year for expenses

NEW YORK

Basic Nursing Scholarships	$200 to $500 per year

ELIGIBILITY	WHERE TO APPLY
Awarded on basis of family income and student's tuition costs	Department of Higher Education Office of Student Financial Aid 225 West State Street Trenton, New Jersey 08625
Child of veteran parent who was killed, or died, as a result of service in the Armed Forces during specified times	Bureau of Veterans' Service Department of Institutions and Agencies Labor and Industry Building, Room 1108 John Fitch Plaza Trenton, New Jersey 08625
Exceptional financial need and academic or creative promise	Office of Student Aid University of New Mexico, Building Y-1 Albuquerque, New Mexico 87106, or the Office of Student Aid at the college you plan to attend
Approval by college, lending institution, and state	Local lending institution, or University of Mexico Office of Student Aid, Building Y-1 Albuquerque, New Mexico 87106
Based on high school performance and need, but granted primarily on basis of academic background	Office of Student Aid, Building Y-1 University of New Mexico Albuquerque, New Mexico 87106
Child, 16 to 26 years of age, of veteran parent who was killed, or died, as a result of service in the Armed Forces of the United States	New Mexico Veterans Service Commission Box 2324 Santa Fe, New Mexico 87501
Awards based on Regents Scholarship, College Qualification Test, and financial need	High school counselor, or The State Education Department Regents Examination and Scholarship Center 99 Washington Avenue Albany, New York 12210

PROGRAM	AMOUNT OF ASSISTANCE
Regents College Scholarships	$250 to $1,000 per year; renewable for 5 years
Regents Grants for Children of Deceased or Disabled Veterans	Up to $450 per year, for 5 years
Regents Scholarships in Cornell University	$100 to $1,000 per year for reduction of tuition
Regents War Service Scholarships for Veterans	$350, but not exceeding cost of tuition and fees
Scholar Incentive Awards	$100 to $600 per year
New York Higher Education Assistance Corporation Student Loans	Up to $1,500 per academic year; up to $1,000 per year for vocational program
State University Scholarships	$200 per year for most students

Awards based on Regents Scholarship, College Qualification Test, and financial need	The State Education Department Regents Examination and Scholarship Center 99 Washington Avenue Albany, New York 12210
Child of (1) veteran parent who died as a result of active duty during World War I, World War II, the Korean Conflict, or since October 1, 1961, or (2) veteran parent who has a current service-connected disability of at least 50 percent incurred during one of these periods	The State Education Department Regents Examination and Scholarship Center 99 Washington Avenue Albany, New York 12210
Meet the requirements for admission to Cornell University; awards based on Regents Scholarship and College Qualification Test, and financial need	The State Education Department Regents Examination and Scholarship Center 99 Washington Avenue Albany, New York 12210
Served in regular active status in the Armed Forces of the United States after October 1, 1961; basis of awards is a competitive examination	High school counselor, or The State Education Department Regents Examination and Scholarship Center 99 Washington Avenue Albany, New York 12210
Family net taxable income balance must not exceed $20,000 per year; awards based on financial need	The State Education Department Regents Examination and Scholarship Center 99 Washington Avenue Albany, New York 12210
New York state residents in full- and at least half-time degree programs or vocational programs	Through a local lending institution participating in the New York Higher Education Assistance Corporation program
Must apply for Scholar Incentive Award first	The State Education Department Regents Examination and Scholarship Center 99 Washington Avenue Albany, New York 12210, or financial aids office of state-operated college you plan to attend

NORTH CAROLINA

PROGRAM	AMOUNT OF ASSISTANCE
Blanchard Scholarships	$200 to $1,200 per year
Children of Deceased or Disabled Veterans	Varies
Guaranteed Loans	Up to $1,500 per year
Herbert Worth Jackson Scholarships	$1,500 per year
James M. Johnston Scholarships	$2,200 per year for residents of North Carolina; $3,700 per year for out-of-state students
Morehead Awards	Up to $2,250 per year
Prospective Teachers' Scholarship Loan Fund	Up to $600 per year; renewable annually

ELIGIBILITY	WHERE TO APPLY
Episcopal divinity students, sons or daughters of Episcopal ministers, or Episcopal descendants of Colonial ancestors; based on financial need	Student Aid Office University of North Carolina 300 Vance Hall Chapel Hill, North Carolina 27514
Child of veteran parent who was killed, or died, as a result of injuries received in World War I, World War II, the Korean Conflict, or the Vietnam Conflict, or who was receiving compensation for service-connected disability at time of his or her death	Department of Veterans' Affairs P. O. Drawer 2626 Raleigh, North Carolina 27611
Approval by college, lending institution, and state or foundation	State Education Assistance Authority 1307 Glenwood Avenue P. O. Box 10887 Raleigh, North Carolina 27605, or College Foundation, Inc. 714 St. Mary's Street Raleigh, North Carolina 27605
Applicants must be male native-born North Carolinians who attain high academic standing	Student Aid Office University of North Carolina 300 Vance Hall Chapel Hill, North Carolina 27514
Primary considerations are academic promise, financial need, leadership ability, and moral character. One half of these awards are reserved for nursing students	Student Aid Office University of North Carolina 300 Vance Hall Chapel Hill, North Carolina 27514
Any male senior attending an accredited North Carolina high school, or 1 of 26 selected preparatory schools; based on demonstrated superior potential	Morehead Foundation P. O. Box 345 Chapel Hill, North Carolina 27514
Resident students who are preparing to teach; repay loan or agree to teach in North Carolina school system equal to time assisted	Prospective Teachers' Scholarship Loan Fund State Department of Public Instruction Raleigh, North Carolina 27602

PROGRAM	AMOUNT OF ASSISTANCE
Rehabilitation Assistance	Tuition costs
Scholarship Loan for Prospective Teachers of the Mentally Retarded	Up to $900 per year; renewable annually

NORTH DAKOTA

Federally Insured Student Loans	Up to $1,500 per year
General State Scholarships	Waiver of fee (about $240 per year)
Indian Scholarships	Up to $1,500 per year
J. F. T. O'Connor Scholarships	$50 to $500 per year
E. J. Larimore and S. P. Mathews Memorial Fund	$50 to $500 per year
North Dakota Nursing Scholarship/ Loans	Up to $1,000 per year for professional nurse student; $300 per year for practical nurse student; $1,800 per year for graduate professional nurse
Veterans of Vietnam Educational Assistance	Reduction in mandatory admission fees at institutions of higher learning in the state

118

ELIGIBILITY	WHERE TO APPLY
Residents who are physically disabled	State Department of Public Instruction Division of Vocational Rehabilitation Raleigh, North Carolina 27602
Resident students who are preparing to teach the mentally retarded	Scholarships for Teachers of the Mentally Retarded State Department of Public Instruction Raleigh, North Carolina 27602
Approval of college, lending institution, and insuring agency	Local lending institution
Awarded on basis of academic aptitude and promise, financial need, citizenship, and character	Student Financial Aids Office University of North Dakota University Station Grand Forks, North Dakota 58201
Be of at least one-quarter degree Indian blood, accepted by an institution of higher learning in North Dakota, have financial need, and indicate probable and continuing success as a student	Executive Director, North Dakota Indian Affairs Commission State Capitol Building Bismarck, North Dakota 58501
Selected on basis of superior academic ability, high qualities of character, and a capacity for leadership	Student Financial Aids Office University of North Dakota University Station Grand Forks, North Dakota 58201
Selected on basis of superior academic ability, high qualities of character, and a capacity for leadership	Student Financial Aids Office University of North Dakota University Station Grand Forks, North Dakota 58201
Be 18 years of age and a legal resident of North Dakota, be accepted into a nursing education program, and show financial need	North Dakota Nursing Scholarship/ Loans Committee 219 North 7th Street Bismarck, North Dakota 58501
Any veteran who served in active duty status in the Armed Forces of the United States for more than 180 days	Department of Veterans Affairs 55½ Broadway P. O. Box 1287 Fargo, North Dakota 58102

PROGRAM	AMOUNT OF ASSISTANCE
Vocational Rehabilitation Program	Tuition, fees, and textbooks
War Orphans' Education Assistance	Financial assistance toward tuition and fees

OHIO

PROGRAM	AMOUNT OF ASSISTANCE
Cooperative Housing Scholarships	Reduction in room and board fees because of the cooperative feature of the program
General University Scholarships	$150 to $1,000 per year
Guaranteed Student Loans	Up to $2,500 per year
Ohio Instructional Grants	$90 to $510 (public institution); $150 to $1,200 (private institution)
War Orphans' Scholarships	Payment of instructional and general fees at state-supported colleges and universities (also includes room and board and books for children of veteran parent who is prisoner of war or missing in action)

ELIGIBILITY	WHERE TO APPLY
Students with a physical limitation or health problem	Division of Vocational Rehabilitation of your nearest district or regional office
Dependents of deceased veterans, or living veterans who have disabilities total and permenant in nature; must have been as result of service in the Armed Forces of the United States	Department of Veterans Affairs 55½ Broadway P. O. Box 1287 Fargo, North Dakota 58102, or any Veterans Administration regional office
Enrolled, or accepted for enrollment, at Ohio State University and acceptance by Scholarship Committee; based on financial need and academic performance	Student Financial Aids Office Ohio State University 154 West 12th Avenue Columbus, Ohio 43210
Enrolled, or accepted for enrollment, at Ohio State University and acceptance by Scholarship Committee; based on financial need and academic performance	Student Financial Aids Office Ohio State University 154 West 12th Avenue Columbus, Ohio 43210
Approval by college, lending institution, and Student Loan Commission	Local lending institution
Awards based on need; must be an Ohio resident	Ohio Board of Regents 88 East Broad Street Columbus, Ohio 43215
Child, 16 to 21 years of age, of veteran parent who entered the Armed Services as a resident of Ohio and is deceased, or 60 percent or greater disabled due to such service during certain periods; or has been declared a prisoner of war or missing in action in Southeast Asia after January 1, 1960	Ohio Board of Regents 88 East Broad Street Columbus, Ohio 43215

OKLAHOMA

PROGRAM	AMOUNT OF ASSISTANCE
General Scholarships	Varies
Guaranteed Student Loans	Up to $1,000 per year
Regents Fee Waiver	Waiver of fees at state-supported institutions of higher learning

OREGON

Four-year State Cash Awards	Up to $500 per year; renewable for 4 years
Guaranteed Student Loans	Up to $1,000 per academic year (undergraduate)
State Need/Grant	Up to $1,000
State Community College Grant	Up to $300

ELIGIBILITY	WHERE TO APPLY
Any prospective full-time student at the University of Oklahoma may apply; based on academic achievement and financial need	Financial Aids Office University of Oklahoma 650 Parrington Oval, Room 302 D Norman, Oklahoma 73069
Approval by college, lending institution, and state	Local lending institution, or Oklahoma State Regents for Higher Education 118 State Capitol Building Oklahoma City, Oklahoma 73105
Based on scholastic achievement and financial need	Oklahoma State Regents for Higher Education 118 State Capitol Building Oklahoma City, Oklahoma 73105, or admissions office of state school the student plans to attend
Awards based on past academic record, promise of success in college, and financial need; must be Oregon resident at a 2- or 4-year degree-granting institution in Oregon	High school counselor, or State Scholarship Commission 1445 Willamette Street Eugene, Oregon 97401
Approval by college, lending institution, and Oregon State Scholarship Commission	Local lending institution
Be an Oregon resident at a 2- or 4-year degree-granting institution in Oregon; based on financial need	High school counselor or principal
Be an Oregon resident at any Oregon community college	High school counselor or principal

PENNSYLVANIA

PROGRAM	AMOUNT OF ASSISTANCE
Guaranteed Student Loans	Up to $1,500 per year
State Scholarships	One third of financial need not to exceed cost of tuition with a maximum of $1,200 in the state of Pennsylvania; $800 out of the state
State Senatorial Scholarships	Partial tuition at a state institution of higher learning
Education for Children of Deceased or Permanently and Totally Disabled Veterans	Up to $200 per term; maximum grant is $1,600 over a 4-year consecutive period

PUERTO RICO

Legislative Scholarships (undergraduates) (a) To attend public institutions of higher learning	(a) Up to $650 per year to attend public colleges
(b) To attend private institutions of higher learning	(b) Varies

124

ELIGIBILITY	WHERE TO APPLY
Approval by college, lending institution, and state	Local lending institution
Awards are based on financial need	High school counselor, office of your local legislator, or Pennsylvania Higher Education Assistance Agency Towne House, 660 Boas Street Harrisburg, Pennsylvania 17102
Awarded by each state senator to an incoming freshman	The state senator from your district
Child, 16 to 21 years of age, of veteran parent who was killed, or died, or was totally disabled during certain war periods; child must be a resident of Pennsylvania for 5 years preceding date of application	Department of Military Affairs Bureau of Veterans Assistance P. O. Box 2769 Harrisburg, Pennsylvania 17105
(a) Awards based on financial need and scholastic achievement	(a) Council on Higher Education University of Puerto Rico Rio Piedras, Puerto Rico 00931
(b) Awards based on financial need and scholastic achievement	(b) Council on Higher Education University of Puerto Rico Rio Piedras, Puerto Rico 00931, or the individual private college the student plans to attend

(The Financial Assistance Program of Puerto Rico is currently under study by the Council on Higher Education, University of Puerto Rico, Rio Piedras, Puerto Rico.)

RHODE ISLAND

PROGRAM	AMOUNT OF ASSISTANCE
Business Education Teachers Scholarship	Varies
Guaranteed Student Loans	Up to $1,500 per year
Nursing Education Scholarships	Varies
State Scholarship Program	$250 to $1,000 per year
War Orphans' Scholarships	Varies

SOUTH CAROLINA

Carolina Scholars	Scholarships that carry a stipend of $1,250 per year
Guaranteed Student Loans	Up to $2,500 per year

126

ELIGIBILITY	WHERE TO APPLY
Plan to become a teacher in the field of business education; agree to teach in Rhode Island schools for at least 2 years, and take qualifying examinations	Dean of Admissions Bryant College 154 Hope Street Providence, Rhode Island 02906, or State Agency for Elementary and Secondary Education Roger Williams Building, Hayes Street Providence, Rhode Island 02908
Approval by college, lending institution, and state	Local lending institution
High school graduates who are of proper age, character, and financial need	College or hospital you plan to attend, or State Agency for Elementary and Secondary Education Roger Williams Building, Hayes Street Providence, Rhode Island 02908
Awarded on basis of scholastic records, test performance, and financial need	State Agency for Elementary and Secondary Education Roger Williams Building, Hayes Street Providence, Rhode Island 02908
Child, 16 to 21 years of age, of a veteran parent who was killed, or died, or was more than 50 percent disabled during any war in which the United States has been engaged	State Agency for Elementary and Secondary Education Roger Williams Building, Hayes Street Providence, Rhode Island 02908
Students who show superior scholastic ability and achievement, leadership, character, and signs of future promise.	Director of Student Financial Aid University of South Carolina Columbia, South Carolina 29208
Approval by college, lending institution, and guarantee agency	Local lending institution, or United Student Aid Funds, Inc. 5259 N. Tacoma Avenue Indianapolis, Indiana 46220

PROGRAM	AMOUNT OF ASSISTANCE
War Orphans' Assistance Program	Waiver of tuition at any of the state-supported colleges or universities

SOUTH DAKOTA

Guaranteed Student Loans	Up to $1,500 per year
Indian Scholarship Program	Tuition waivers at state-supported institution of higher learning
Veterans' and War Orphans' Assistance Program	Waiver of tuition at state-supported colleges and universities

TENNESSEE

Academic Scholarships	Varies
Guaranteed Student Loans	Up to $1,000 per year
War Orphans' Assistance Program	Tuition scholarships at state-supported colleges and universities

ELIGIBILITY	WHERE TO APPLY
Child of a war veteran who is permanently and totally disabled from any cause or if the veteran-father died from a service-connected disability	Department of Veterans Affairs 1015 Main Street Columbia, South Carolina 29201
Approval by college, lending institution, and insuring agency	Local lending institution
Must be a certified Indian resident of South Dakota and accepted at a 4-year college or university	Regents of Education State of South Dakota Capitol Building Pierre, South Dakota 57501, or the college the student plans to attend
Veterans who were honorably discharged, if not receiving federal educational assistance, and children of veterans who were killed or died during certain war periods	Regents of Education State of South Dakota Capitol Building Pierre, South Dakota 57501
Outstanding high school graduates are considered	The state college or university the student plans to attend
Approval by college, lending institution, and state	Local lending institution, or Tennessee Educational Loan Corporation 313 Capitol Towers Nashville, Tennessee 37219

Child of veteran parent who died as a result of (or was killed) serving in the Armed Forces during certain periods	State Department of Education
	100 Cordell Hull Building
	Nashville, Tennessee 37219, or
	    the state college or university the
	    student plans to attend

TEXAS

PROGRAM	AMOUNT OF ASSISTANCE
Connally-Carrillo Scholarships	Tuition waivers and partial fee exemptions
Guaranteed Student Loans	Up to $1,000 per year
Nursing Stipends	Varies
Orphans' Educational Assistance Program	Waivers of tuition and fees at state colleges
Veterans' and War Orphans' Assistance Program	Tuition and fees

UTAH

Guaranteed Student Loans	Up to $1,500 per year
Honors at Entrance Scholarships	Tuition

ELIGIBILITY	WHERE TO APPLY

Based on class rank or test scores, and must come from a family with an income of less than $4,800	Coordinating Board
	Texas College and University System
	Sam Houston State Office Building
	Austin, Texas 78711, or
	    office of student financial aid
	    at the college or university the student
	    plans to attend

Approval of college, lending institution, and state	Coordinating Board
	Texas College and University System
	Sam Houston State Office Building
	Austin, Texas 78711, or
	    office of student financial aid at
	    the college or university the student
	    plans to attend

Qualified students who pursue nursing at Prairie View A and M College	Prairie View A and M College Prairie View, Texas 77445
High school graduates who were boarded at Texas orphanages; orphans of certain National Guard and Air National Guard personnel are eligible also	Coordinating Board Texas College and University System Sam Houston State Office Building Austin, Texas 78711

Certain veterans and children of certain deceased veterans are eligible	Coordinating Board
	Texas College and University System
	Sam Houston State Office Building
	Austin, Texas 78711, or
	    the state college the student plans to
	    attend

Approval by college, lending institution, and federal government	Local lending institution, or the college the student plans to attend
Selected on the basis of scholastic achievement and residency in Utah	Financial Aids and Scholarships Office The University of Utah Salt Lake City, Utah 84112

PROGRAM	AMOUNT OF ASSISTANCE
Leadership Scholarships	Tuition
Presidential Honor Scholarships	Tuition and registration fee
Tuition Scholarships	Waiver of registration and tuition fees in full or in part
War Orphans' Assistance Program	Tuition, books, and supplies at state college

VERMONT

War Orphans' Assistance	Varies

VIRGINIA

Guaranteed Student Loans	Up to $1,000 per year for undergraduates; $2,000 for graduates
Nursing Scholarships	$300 each

Students who have demonstrated out-standing capabilities as student leaders in Utah high schools; and residency in Utah	Financial Aids and Scholarships Office The University of Utah Salt Lake City, Utah 84112
Exceptionally well-qualified students	Financial Aids and Scholarships Office The University of Utah Salt Lake City, Utah 84112
Scholastic achievement and financial need	Chairman, Scholarship, Awards, and Honors Committee Utah State University Logan, Utah 84321
Children and unremarried widows of certain veterans who were killed or died as a result of military service	State Superintendent of Public Instruction 1400 University Club Building 136 East South Temple Salt Lake City, Utah 84111
Children of veterans who were killed or died as a result of service during certain war periods	State Department of Education Montpelier, Vermont 05602
Virginia students in approved Virginia schools or in accredited colleges and universities out-of-state, if also approved by U. S. Office of Education	Local Virginia lending institution that participates in the Virginia Guaranteed Student Loan Program
Resident student nurses at approved Virginia schools for nursing who agree to practice 1 year in Virginia for each year of assistance	State Board of Health Richmond, Virginia 23219

PROGRAM	AMOUNT OF ASSISTANCE
Virginia Teachers' Scholarship/Loan Program	$450 annually at 6 percent interest
Virginia World War Orphans' Education Benefits	Free tuition in state institutions; may also include other limited expenditures

WASHINGTON

Assistance for the Blind	Tuition and laboratory fees exemption; financial assistance not to exceed $200 per quarter
Children of Veterans	Exemptions from payment of tuition fees at state institutions of higher learning

WEST VIRGINIA

Federal Loan Program	Up to $1,500 per year
West Virginia Scholarship Program	$100 to $900 per academic year

ELIGIBILITY	WHERE TO APPLY
Good students who are graduates of Virginia high schools, who plan to attend a Virginia college or university and pursue an approved teacher-education program (in fields of shortages)	The college or university in Virginia the student plans to attend
Child, 16 to 25 years of age, whose parent was a Virginia citizen at time of entering service who was killed, died or was totally and permanently disabled as a result of service in the Armed Forces of the United States during certain periods of war, or who was listed as missing in action or a prisoner of war	Director, Division of War Veterans Claims 211 West Campbell Avenue Roanoke, Virginia 24011
Must be in financial need, be legally blind, and be admitted to an institution of higher learning	State Board of Education Old Capitol Building Olympia, Washington 98504
Children, 16 to 22, resident 1 year, of veteran parent who was killed, or died, or was totally incapacitated as a result of service in the Armed Forces of the United States	State Board of Education Old Capitol Building Olympia, Washington 98504
Any student who is enrolled or accepted for enrollment at a college, university, or vocational school on at least a half-time basis; the loan is subject to approval by the college, lending institution, and U. S. Office of Education	Local lending institution, or West Virginia Board of Regents 1316 Charleston National Plaza Charleston, West Virginia 25301
Awards based on academic promise as well as academic achievement, financial need, good moral character, and residency in West Virginia	High school principal, or West Virginia Scholarship Program West Virginia Commission on Higher Education 1316 Charleston National Plaza Charleston, West Virginia 25301

PROGRAM	AMOUNT OF ASSISTANCE
War Orphans' Education Program	Waiver of tuition at West Virginia state institution of higher education; some students also qualify for monetary aid to help defray costs of room, board, books, etc.

WISCONSIN

Economic Assistance Loans	Up to $2,000 per year
Honor Scholarships	Up to $800, freshman year only
Part-time Study Grants	Reimbursement of cost of fees and text-books upon satisfactory completion of part-time classroom study or correspondence courses from an approved school
Guaranteed Student Loans	Up to $1,000 per year
Wisconsin Tuition Grant Program	Up to $900 per year for freshmen; $650 for sophomores, juniors, and seniors.

Child, 16 to 23 years of age, of veteran parent who was killed or died as a result of injuries received during certain war periods	West Virginia Department of Veterans' Affairs State Capitol Building Charleston, West Virginia 25305
Certain veterans, unmarried widows, and minor or dependent children of deceased veterans, or a remarried widow for the education of a veteran's minor or dependent children if the widow is a resident of the state; also based on financial need	County Veterans' Service Office Courthouse, County Seat Each county in Wisconsin
Wisconsin high school seniors in the top 10 percent of the graduating class; the number of scholarships awarded in each high school is based on total enrollment; financial need is a consideration	Wisconsin Honor Scholarship Program Higher Educational Aids Board 115 West Wilson Street Madison, Wisconsin 53703
Veterans, widows, minor or dependent children of deceased Wisconsin veterans of any war, if residents of, and living in, Wisconsin at time of application	County Veterans' Service Office State of Wisconsin Department of Veterans Affairs Room 700, 1 West Wilson Street Madison, Wisconsin 53702

Any student enrolled or accepted for enrollment at a college or university; the loan is subject to approval by the college, lending institution, and the state	Local lending institution, or
	   financial aids office at the college
	   you attend, or plan to attend, or
	Wisconsin Higher Education
	   Corporation
	115 West Wilson Street
	Madison, Wisconsin 53703

Based on financial need; must be a resident of Wisconsin in full-time attendance at an eligible institution, and be in good academic standing	State of Wisconsin Higher Educational Aids Board 115 West Wilson Street Madison, Wisconsin 53703

WYOMING

PROGRAM	AMOUNT OF ASSISTANCE
Guaranteed Student Loans	Varies
Honor Scholarships	$111 per semester at the University of Wyoming
War Orphans' Assistance Program	Usually covers tuition and fees

ELIGIBILITY	WHERE TO APPLY
Student enrolled, or accepted for enrollment, at a college or university; loan is subject to approval by the college, lending institution, and state	Local lending institution, or the financial aids office of the college or university the student plans to attend
Graduating Wyoming high school seniors; based on academic performance and need	High school principal or counselor
Certain war orphans whose eligibility is verified by the Federal Veterans Administration Center	Federal Veterans Administration Center Cheyenne, Wyoming 82001